CHRISTIAN HEROES: THEN & NOW

Adoniram Judson
Amy Carmichael
Betty Greene
Brother Andrew
Cameron Townsend
Charles Mulli
Clarence Jones
Corrie ten Boom
Count Zinzendorf
C. S. Lewis
C. T. Studd
David Bussau
David Livingstone
D. L. Moody
Elisabeth Elliot
Eric Liddell
Florence Young
Francis Asbury
George Müller
Gladys Aylward
Hudson Taylor
Ida Scudder
Isobel Kuhn

Jacob DeShazer
Jim Elliot
John Flynn
John Wesley
John Williams
Jonathan Goforth
Klaus-Dieter John
Lillian Trasher
Loren Cunningham
Lottie Moon
Mary Slessor
Mildred Cable
Nate Saint
Paul Brand
Rachel Saint
Richard Wurmbrand
Rowland Bingham
Samuel Zwemer
Sundar Singh
Wilfred Grenfell
William Booth
William Carey

Available in paperback, e-book, and audiobook formats.
Unit Study Curriculum Guides are available for select biographies.
www.HeroesThenAndNow.com

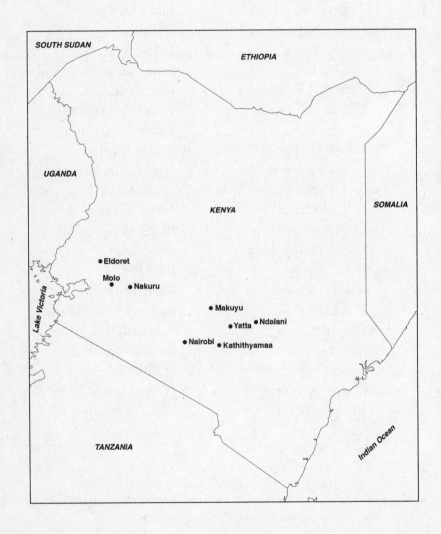

Contents

Chapter 1

Left Behind

Charles Mulli awoke to sunlight filtering through cracks in the thatched grass roof of his family's mud hut. His neck still hurt from the beating his father had given him two nights before. Thankfully last night his father had collapsed onto his bed, too drunk to even throw a punch at Charles's mother. Charles could hear the hen pecking outside the door, the same hen his parents had consulted yesterday. As far as Charles could understand, his father, Daudi, believed that when he prayed to the hen, his ancestors would hear him and bless and guide him. The prayers had lasted for a long time, and when they were over, Charles's father strode off with a determined look on his face.

The hen stopped pecking, and suddenly Charles was aware that the hut was silent—totally silent. There was not even the rustle of his mother, Rhoda, moving about the hut preparing to light the fire to cook *ugali*, or the babbling of his one-year-old sister, Katumbi. Ignoring the pain, Charles lifted his head and looked around. Except for himself, the bed he shared with his younger brothers, Musyoka and Dickson, was empty. Stranger still, the hut was empty.

Charles quickly sat up on the edge of the bed, wide awake. What had happened? Where was his family? How had he slept through the commotion of everyone getting up and leaving? Charles forced himself to think. There was something different, something alarming about the situation. Charles swung his feet to the floor, stood up, and opened the door. He didn't need to change out of the ripped shirt and pants he had slept in, since they were the only clothes he owned.

Charles walked out into the bright African morning, past the acacia trees, and along the edge of the track that led to the maize field. He tried to reassure himself that his family had gotten an early start working in the field. But he could see no one bending over to weed the maize crop. His heart pounded in his chest as he took off running along the track to his grandmother's hut. Would his grandmother be there? Was anyone left to take care of him?

It normally took ten minutes for Charles to reach his grandmother's house from the maize field, but this morning he covered the distance in record time. He almost wept for joy when he saw his grandmother sitting on a stool slicing beans with a long knife. She looked up wearily when she saw him approaching.

"Father and Mother are not in the hut. Do you know where they are?" an out-of-breath Charles asked.

His grandmother sighed deeply before answering. "They have gone, Charles, and they have left you behind."

"Just for the day? They'll be back, won't they?"

Charles's grandmother shook her head as a chilling thought overcame Charles. Somewhere deep inside he knew his family was gone, not for a day or a week but for good. It was no accident he had slept through it all. His father, mother, and brothers had all conspired to leave him behind. Perhaps that was what the ancestors had told his father to do when he had prayed to the hen the day before.

This was a lot for a six-year-old boy to absorb. Charles stood by the door of his grandmother's hut trying to sort through the information. "What will happen to me?" he asked.

His grandmother wiped a tear from her wrinkled face. "You will live with me, but . . ." Her voice trailed off.

Charles knew very well what the *but* meant. They lived in Kathithyamaa, the village in south central Kenya where his mother and her brothers had been raised. According to local custom, the brothers stayed with the parents and inherited the land, while the sisters were married off and moved away to their husbands' lands. A daughter had no right to inherit anything from her parents. But Daudi Mulli had broken with tradition and come to stay with his wife's family, bringing along Charles and their other three children. Rhoda Mulli's five brothers, Charles's uncles, resented the fact that their sister had returned home and expected them to help support her, her husband, and the children. Charles had once over-heard Uncle Nzioka arguing with his grandmother about giving the Mulli family food from her tiny garden. Charles knew that his uncles would be very angry that he had been left behind, fearing that he would grow up there and be entitled to some of their inheritance.

Charles gathered a sack to sleep on from the old family hut and carried it to his grandmother's place, his new home. His grandmother's hut was even smaller than the one the Mulli family had been living in, but it felt like a safe haven to Charles. In Charles's previous experience, his father would beat his mother more nights than not and then unleash his fury on Charles and his brothers. It felt good to him to sleep in the corner of the hut knowing he would not be sub-jected to another nightmarish beating.

Soon, however, a new nightmare presented itself. The reality in his new home of feeding two mouths instead of one became urgent. There was no food left in his grandmother's hut, and her tiny garden didn't produce enough vegetables to feed them both. Some-times her sons brought food, staying to watch her eat it and insisting she not share any of it with Charles. "Let him beg," they said. "His parents left him behind. He is worthless. We don't want him either."

Charles recoiled at the idea of begging. It was bad enough that the other children in the village taunted him with "Bure Bure" (unwanted orphan). What would they say when he started begging for food from their families?

After not eating for three and a half days, Charles broke down and headed to a neighbor to ask for food. Despite the hunger gnawing at his stomach, he hated what he was being forced to do. Luckily a kind woman was in the first hut, and she gave him boiled manioc to eat. She even knelt beside Charles to talk to him, but he ran away before she could ask him any questions.

Charles made the manioc last for two days and then had to beg again. Sometimes he met with kindness, but as the months went by, many people became weary of feeding the six-year-old who had been left behind. "What's wrong with you? Why didn't your family take you with them? Why did they take the others and leave you behind?" they would ask him.

Charles didn't know how to answer the questions. He had heard a rumor that his parents and siblings were in Kenya's capital, Nairobi, thirty-five miles to the west. Sometimes at night as he lay on his sack in the corner of his grandmother's hut, he tried to imagine what might be happening in the capital. What were his brothers doing? Were they rich enough to go to school? Had his father found a job and stopped drinking and beating his mother? A year passed, and still Charles's parents did not return. He had become used to his new life, even though each day was a struggle.

Another year passed. Charles was now eight years old and felt like an old man. Every day he was burdened with the need to find enough food to fend off starvation. He was sure that his life would not only never get any better but would also get worse when his grandmother died and he was left completely alone. But late one afternoon as Charles was weeding his grandmother's small garden, a boy from the village came running up to him. "Come quickly! She's here!" he yelled.

"Who's here?" Charles asked.

"Your mother. Your mother is back."

"Where?"

"At your grandmother's hut," the boy said.

Charles took off running.

As he rounded the corner on the track to his grandmother's hut, Charles saw a cluster of relatives around the doorway. Four of his uncles and several of his cousins were there, and they all looked somber. Charles didn't stop to talk to them. He wanted to see his mother more than anything in the world. As Charles ran past the relatives, Uncle Kaisi reached out to grab him, but Charles pulled away and dashed inside. His eyes took a moment to adjust to the dim interior of the hut from the bright sun outside. His grandmother sat on her old stool, and a woman lay on the floor, slumped over against the opposite wall. Charles stared. Was the woman on the floor his mother? He looked closer but could barely recognize her. The woman's eyes were bruised and swollen almost completely shut. Her head was swollen almost to the size of a large melon, and her face bore a patchwork of cuts and bruises.

The sight of his mother's condition made Charles want to vomit. Only one person could have done such a terrible thing to her, and that was his father. Charles's hands balled into fists as rage filled his heart. He wished his father were there right then so he could fight him.

"Hello, Charles?" his mother whispered.

Charles ignored her. He was too angry to speak, angry that she had stayed with his father, angry that he could not protect her, and angry that she had left him behind. Then he heard a whimper from a pile of rags in the corner that he hadn't noticed. He turned to see his grandmother pick something up. It was a baby. Charles stepped over to take a better look. "This is your brother Zachariah," his grandmother said.

As he looked closer, Charles saw that the skin around the baby's hands and the back of his head was raw and seeping yellow fluid. "What's wrong with him?" he asked, afraid of the answer he would get.

His grandmother sighed. "Your mother says Daudi attacked her, but this time she had the baby in her arms. She tried to shield the baby, but during the beating, the child slipped from her hands and into the fire."

Charles stared blankly at his mother. Would the nightmare never end?

Uncle Nzioka stepped inside the hut. Rhoda looked up at him. "I need to get to the hospital, at least for the sake of the baby," she pleaded through blood-dried, swollen lips.

Uncle Nzioka helped Charles's mother to her feet. He then led her, clutching Zachariah, out of the hut.

That night, lying on his sack on the floor, Charles thought about his mother in the hospital. As he listened to his grandmother's labored breathing, he tried to process the events of the day. Had his mother come home to die? And brought Zachariah with her? What if she died in the hospital and the baby lived? Who would look after him? Would Charles be responsible for the baby? And if his mother did recover, would she leave again? And would she take Charles with her this time? Charles had many more questions than answers. As was usually the case, he knew he would have to wait to see what fate sent his way.

As time passed, Charles begged his grandmother for news of his mother and baby brother. All she told him was that they were still in the hospital. At last his mother returned to his grandmother's hut with Zachariah. This time Charles immediately recognized her. She looked much better and even gave him a hug. Zachariah's hands and head were healing too, with the help of the ointment that was rubbed on his wounds every morning and evening.

After his mother's return to Kathithyamaa, questions continued to plague Charles: What would happen next? Would his mother creep out in the night and return to his monster of a father? And if so, would she take the baby with her? Surely, Charles thought, she would not go back to his father after her latest beating.

As it turned out, Daudi came to Rhoda. One day about a month later, he appeared at the door of Charles's grandmother's hut. Charles instantly recognized his father's short, muscular frame at the door and tried to shrink from his sight. He needn't have bothered. His father totally ignored him as he stepped inside.

It did not take long for word to spread throughout Kathithyamaa about Daudi's return. Soon the hut was crowded with uncles. Charles was told to step outside, though he could still hear everything that was going on inside.

"You should be ashamed leaving that boy to fend for himself," one uncle said.

"We know what you are up to. You cannot come back here to live. We don't want you," another said. "And if you don't take better care of your wife, we will report you to the clan elders."

Charles found satisfaction in thinking about that possibility. He knew that the clan elders stepped in to hear only serious offenses, but when they did, justice was swift and severe.

Daudi's voice was low and calm. "That's behind me now. I wouldn't have come back if I didn't want to take responsibility for my family."

"What about Charles?" Uncle Kingoo interjected.

"Yes, him too. Charles is my oldest son, and I will take him to Molo, where the rest of the family are waiting. We should never have left him behind."

Charles's heart sank as he heard these words. How could he endure another round of drunken violence? It was much better to stay with his mother and grandmother, even if food was scarce. Fear of the future began gnawing at Charles's soul as surely as hunger gnawed at his stomach.

The conversation inside his grandmother's hut went on and on, and Charles could sense that his father was wearing his mother's relatives down. At last Uncle Ndambuki said, "All right, you can leave with Rhoda, but you must keep your promise to mend your ways. And you must take the boy with you."

Charles knew there was no point in arguing. His fate was sealed.

The following morning the Mulli family—including Charles—were up early. It was time to leave. A knot the size of a mango had settled in Charles's stomach. The night before, his mother had told him they would take a bus to Nairobi and then another bus to the village of Molo in the Rift Valley. That was where his mother had been beaten and where his two brothers remained working at the Kavulu farm, owned by a rich white farmer. His mother had still more news for him. She informed Charles that his little sister Katumbi had died of a fever. Charles was shocked. What else regarding the move to Molo didn't he know about?

The Familiar Knot

Charles peered out of the bus window. He was on his way one hundred miles northwest of Nairobi to Molo, to a white man's farm where his family worked. As the arid red landscape flashed by, Charles hoped for a new beginning. Even though he found it hard to believe, he hoped that his father meant what he said, that the seriousness of his mother's last beating and the burns on Zachariah made him permanently want to change his ways. Charles also hoped that his mother would keep her promise that he could go to school at Molo.

It was late afternoon when the bus dropped off the Mulli family at the bus stop nearest to the Kavulu farm. But the family still had seven miles to walk. They did not have much to carry. Charles's mother slung Zachariah on her back, and his father carried a sack holding a few vegetables. Charles had a small bag of salt his grandmother had given him.

As the sun sank, Charles followed his father along a path between white chrysanthemums that bloomed as far as he could see. "They use the seeds in the flowers to make a liquid that keeps insects away from plants," Charles's mother told him. A little farther on she announced, "We are nearly there."

Sure enough, Charles soon spotted three mud huts in a field. They looked the same as the huts at Kathithyamaa, with their mud walls, thatched grass roofs, and holes for windows. Just a few yards away, two young boys were digging holes for planting. "Musyoka! Dickson!" Charles yelled, running toward them. The three brothers hugged each other and danced around. Charles turned to see his parents grinning. *Perhaps,* he allowed himself to think, *this really will be a new beginning for us all.*

"I will boil some vegetables," his mother said, and to her husband she added, "You take Charles to his grandfather."

Charles's father nodded. "You will have to stay there. There's not enough room in the hut for all of us," he told Charles.

Charles felt fear rising in his chest. He could not remember Kaleli, his father's father. What if Kaleli was like his father? Or even worse? Was the nightmare about to begin all over again?

It was dusk when they arrived at grandfather Kaleli's hut. He was a strong man and very dark, like Charles's father, with gleaming white teeth.

"I heard you were coming. I'm glad you are here,"

his grandfather said, encircling Charles with a firm hug. Charles was stunned. In his whole life he could not remember anyone saying he was glad to see him. Perhaps things would be better here than he had dared imagine.

Charles and his two brothers played outside while his father and Kaleli talked inside. Then it was time for them all to go, leaving Charles alone with the old man.

"Sit here," Kaleli said. "You must be hungry."

Charles grinned. How good it felt to be offered food instead of having to beg for it.

Soon the two of them were sitting side by side, Kaleli on a three-legged stool and Charles on an upturned tree trunk.

"How old are you, boy?" Kaleli asked.

"Nine years old," Charles replied as he scooped up another mouthful of delicious sweet potato.

"Ah, when I was that age, my grandfather used to tell me stories. Would you like to hear one?"

His mouth full, Charles nodded.

"A long, long time ago, there was a very poor little boy named Chochote. He had nothing, and he decided to leave his land in search of a better life. Chochote built a boat and sailed across the water. After many days he saw a small island and went ashore. There he found a wonderful paradise—with many fruit trees and happy people. He met a beautiful girl, the daughter of the king, walking along the beach, and they fell in love."

Charles took another mouthful of food. He was amazed that his grandfather was telling him a story. No one had ever done that for him before.

Kaleli went on. "Of course, the king did not want his daughter to marry such a poor man, a man with nothing. But the princess loved Chochote, and eventually the king gave his permission for the marriage. 'But first let us visit your family,' the king said. Chochote worried that the king would change his mind if he saw how desperately poor his family was, but the king insisted. He called for his big boat, and the whole royal family, along with Chochote, set off across the water. They came to the village where Chochote's family lived. They were now even poorer than when he had left. Their crops had failed, and no rain had fallen for months.

"When the king saw all of this, he said to the family, 'If Chochote is to be my son-in-law, you are also my people. Come aboard my boat. I will take you all back to the island, and you can live with us.' Chochote could hardly believe his ears. But the king made it so. He took the whole family to the island, where they grew strong and happy, and Chochote and the princess lived happily too."

Charles sat smiling. He was delighted to have a full stomach and a story in his head. "Do you know more stories like that?" he asked.

Kaleli chuckled. "Many more. My grandfather told me many stories. I will tell them to you also. But not now. It is time now to go to sleep."

Charles lay down on a pile of sacks. Although he could feel the bumps on the ground beneath him, he was happy. He drifted off to sleep, thinking about Chochote and the princess. How wonderful it would be if a king came and took his whole family to a beautiful island where there was food for everyone.

The following morning, wearing a big smile, Rhoda said to her son, "Come with me, Charles. I am taking you to school."

Charles could hardly believe his ears. Really? School? Where he could learn to read and write? His mind whirled with possibilities. Perhaps one day he would be able to read stories like the one Kaleli had told him the night before.

"Put on these clothes," his mother said, handing Charles a gray shirt with buttons and a pair of khaki shorts. They weren't new, of course, but they were clean and tidy.

Charles stared at them for a minute, taking it all in. He had a uniform. It was difficult to believe. He really was going to school!

Charles and his mother, who carried Zachariah bundled on her back, set out walking along the road to the west. After about a mile, Charles spotted a long, low building with mud walls and a corrugated metal roof. School at last! As they got closer, inside he could see rows of wooden benches with long stools under them and a very tall man standing at the front of the classroom with a stick in his hand. "That is your teacher," his mother said. "Do what he says, or you will get into trouble."

Charles didn't need to be told that. He had dreamed of going to school for as long as he could remember. His father had attended school to second grade, and his mother to third grade. They could read and write simple sentences in Kikamba, their language, but neither of them knew a word of English. Charles dreamed of a time when he would be able to read and write in English and in Kikamba.

The teacher, Mr. Jengo, pointed to a bench, and Charles squeezed onto the end of it. Three other boys were already sitting there, all sharing one Swahili reading book. Although not Charles's native language, Swahili was the official language of Kenya, and every student learned it in school. Charles did not have a pencil or notebook, and so he had to be content to watch as the other students wrote things down. He hoped his mother would buy him school supplies soon.

It didn't take Charles long to realize that Mr. Jengo was a violent man, who lashed out when the children did not obey his commands. Because of the beatings from his father over the years, Charles had been left partially deaf and did not always understand what the teacher said. As a result, he often felt the crack of Mr. Jengo's rod over his head. Despite this, Charles was grateful to be at school. He especially loved mathematics and soon learned to add and subtract numbers up to one hundred.

Sometimes after school Charles ate with his family, but most often Kaleli provided his meals. When Charles did visit his family's hut, he was always on the lookout for signs that his father had been on a violent rampage. Sadly, there were many. His father often left for days looking for work and came back with no money and no patience. Charles also noticed the marks on his mother's face and legs, and his brothers, Musyoka and Dickson, told Charles how their father beat them too. While Charles felt safe with his grandfather, what use was that if the rest of his family was in danger?

One morning when Charles arrived at school, several of the children pointed at him and started whispering to each other. He wondered what had happened. He soon found out. During the night, his father had returned to Molo very drunk and started a fight with a neighbor. It was a big fight, and neither man would give in. Eventually Daudi gained the upper hand and beat his opponent senseless. Then he turned his fury on Rhoda and on Charles's brothers. When he learned what had happened, Charles excused himself from school and ran down the road toward the hut where his parents lived. As his bare feet raced along, he wished he were bigger—big enough to give his father the beating he deserved.

Breathless, Charles stopped in front of the hut. Immediately the familiar knot grew in his stomach. The hut was empty, not just of people but also of belongings. He ran on to Kaleli's hut. His grandfather enveloped him in a hug and then spat on the ground. "Your father is useless," he said. "He has gone and taken the children. Your mother has gone too, back to Kathithyamaa to be taken care of by her mother."

The news felt like a physical punch to Charles. Once again his family was gone, leaving him behind. It was as if all the color had been drained from Charles's world. He still went to school, but now the children taunted him, calling him an orphan, a forgotten one. And Kaleli changed too. He began to drink, and although he was not violent like Charles's father, Kaleli's drinking frightened Charles.

About six months after his family left, Kaleli motioned for Charles to sit beside him outside the hut. It was a cloudless afternoon, but Charles's stomach knotted. Something bad was about to happen—he could feel it.

"I've had word from your father," his grandfather began. "Your mother is better now, and everyone is living together in Nakuru. I am not able to take care of you any longer, Charles. You will have to go to your parents."

"But my parents don't want me. They left me behind, remember?" Charles replied.

"Even so, I cannot take care of you anymore. It is not possible. You are your parents' responsibility. They have to take care of you, and you have to find them. They said they were in Nakuru. I'm sure you will find them there."

"How will I get there?" Charles asked.

"I will give you money for the train, and when you get to Nakuru, you will get off and find some way to contact them."

Charles sat in stunned silence.

"You will find a way, and they will take you in. There is no other way," his grandfather said.

A million objections surfaced in Charles's mind, but he could see it was useless to argue. Grandfather Kaleli had made up his mind. For better or worse,

Charles was about to strike out on his own. "When do I have to go?" he asked.

"In the morning I will walk with you to the train station."

Charles nodded. He doubted he would ever see his grandfather again. And there would be no more school. No more lying down at night and waking up safe in the morning.

That night Charles hardly slept. He ran through all sorts of scenarios in his head, trying to imagine what would happen when he got off the train at Nakuru. Would there be someone who could tell him the way to his parents' house? Would there be some kind merchants who might give him a few food scraps?

In the morning Kaleli hardly spoke. As they walked together the five miles to the train station, Charles thanked his grandfather for taking care of him and for all the wonderful stories of Africa he had told him. "I will never forget them or you as long as I live," he told the old man.

Kaleli nodded and brushed the top of Charles's head with his hand. "You're not a big boy for eleven, but you are strong and determined. You will make a way. I know you will," he said.

Chapter 3

"He's a Waste"

A ll worries about what lay ahead were set aside
when Charles saw the massive steam locomotive come around the bend and shudder to a halt in
front of him. Steam hissed from beneath it, and black
smoke billowed from the stack. It was the biggest
machine Charles had ever seen, and he was about to
ride on it!

Kaleli handed the conductor a ticket, and Charles
climbed aboard the train. He found a seat by the
window, next to man smoking a cigarette. Charles
settled in for the thirty-mile journey to Nakuru. The
locomotive hissed loudly, and the train jerked as it
moved forward. Charles waved to his grandfather
as the train gathered speed. Now he was entirely on
his own. If anything happened to him, neither his

grandfather nor his mother would come looking for him, since each would think he was with the other. Charles tried not to think about that.

Bush and fields passed by the window of the carriage. As he caught glimpses of gazelles and giraffes, Charles marveled at how different it was to travel by train than by bus. For one thing, the train was not as crowded as the bus. In addition, a cool breeze came in through the carriage window. Charles settled back into his seat and tried to relax, but he couldn't. His mind was a tumultuous sea of worries about what would happen to him next and what he would do once he reached Nakuru. How would he find his family? What if his father had up and moved the family away overnight, as he had done before? Did he even want to see his father again?

The man in the seat next to Charles stood and pulled down a small suitcase from the overhead rack. As he opened it, Charles could see that it was packed with books and clothes. The man shuffled among them and pulled out a package of bread and *muthura* (goat sausage). Charles's mouth watered as he watched the man eat. He knew that his grandfather had spent his last shilling on the train ticket and that there had been no money left over for food. Hunger pangs gnawed at Charles's stomach. He wondered what it would be like to be important enough to carry his own suitcase with food and books and clothes inside it. When a woman came through the train selling hot tea, Charles shook his head, while the man next to him bought a cup for himself.

As the man drank his tea, more doubts and concerns surfaced in Charles's mind. Charles had pinned all his hopes on doing well at school, but now, at eleven years of age, he felt that that was behind him. Would he ever go back to school? And if he didn't, what kind of life would he have? If his father did not sober up and stop his violent ways, what hope was there for any of them? Still worse was the thought of not finding his family. If life had been harsh with them, he knew it would be even harsher if he was alone with no one at all to notice whether he lived or died.

Whenever the train hissed to a stop at a station along the way, women would crowd around outside the windows holding up fruit and bread for sale. Charles looked hungrily at the food.

At last, the train conductor walked through the carriage yelling, "Nakuru station! Nakuru station coming up!" This was the end of the journey for Charles. He stood and walked down the aisle. When the train jerked to a halt, he climbed down onto the station platform, where he stood feeling completely alone— alone in a sea of people. Everyone else seemed to have something to do. Men carried luggage through the station doors, and women followed along behind, holding their children's hands.

Within minutes the train had loaded more passengers and luggage and moved on. The station platform was empty except for Charles. The sun beat down overhead. Charles remembered Kaleli telling him that Nakuru was right near the equator. He wiped his forehead with his sleeve and went inside the station. A clerk sat behind a desk. "Excuse me. Do you know where Daudi and Rhoda Mulli live?" Charles asked him.

The clerk looked up and shook his head. "Never heard of them," he said.

Charles walked back out into the sunlight. He had about five hours to find his family before night fell. He saw two men unloading barrels and asked them about his parents. The men simply shrugged. Charles kept walking and, as he made his way through town, asked people if they knew his parents.

For the first hour or so, Charles worked hard to buoy up his optimism. It was just a matter of time, he told himself, before someone recognized the names and could point him in the right direction to find his family. By the time he made it to the market, people were beginning to close their stalls for the day. Charles kept asking those he found in the market if they knew his parents. Some people refused to talk to him, mistaking him for a beggar, he supposed, while others listened politely but could offer little help.

As he watched the sun set over the now-empty marketplace, Charles had still not found his parents. He was unsure what to do and eventually retraced his steps to the train station, where he found a corner on the concrete platform to curl up. He heard light rain tapping on the corrugated metal roof as he slept fitfully through the night. He was up at dawn asking everyone—passersby, drivers of cars that stopped at intersections, shopkeepers, and marketeers—if they had heard of Daudi and Rhoda Mulli. No one had.

It was as if his parents had disappeared from the face of the earth. He saw a boy, just a little bigger than him, pulling food scraps from a garbage can. So Charles checked the next can he came to, and the one after that, hoping to find food. He picked out a piece of meat crawling with maggots. He dropped it back in the can. He was not hungry enough to eat it, at least not yet. A woman with a fruit stand offered him a bruised banana. He took it gratefully and devoured it.

Charles slept another night at the train station. He wished he could get back on the train and return to his grandfather, but he knew he would not be welcome. Besides, he didn't have a penny toward the price of a ticket. For better or for worse, Nakuru was now his home.

Charles realized that he was getting nowhere on his own and that he needed someone to help him in the search for his parents. He changed tactics, asking people if they knew somewhere he could go for help in finding his missing parents. Someone pointed to a police station.

Charles wasn't sure whether this was a good idea. He had never talked to a policeman before, and the police had a reputation for being callous or even abusive toward children. Still, he understood that he had to do something before he became lost in the crowd, just another penniless kid begging on the street. He took a deep breath and entered the police station. An officer walked up to him and asked, "What do you want?" Charles was relieved. The man's voice did not sound cruel. Charles told the officer that he was looking for his parents and that he thought they were working for a white farmer.

"You stay here," the officer said after questioning Charles. "I will go and see if I can find out anything about them."

Charles spent the longest five hours of his life waiting for the police officer to return. He tried not to think the worst, but old fears invaded his mind. What if he didn't find his parents? What if they were dead? Or moved on? What if his father had killed his mother and gone into hiding? What then? He would be an eleven-year-old boy in a strange town with no one at all to rely on.

When the police officer returned, the smile on his face sent a wave of relief through Charles. "I have located them. Follow me," he said.

Charles followed the officer out the door and across the street. They walked for a mile or so to the outskirts of town, where a long row of mud huts stood.

"That one," the police officer said, pointing. "That's where the Mullis live."

After thanking the officer, Charles walked toward the hut. His stomach ached from hunger, and his nerves were on edge. He knocked on the door. No one answered. He knocked again. He heard footsteps. The door opened, and there stood his mother. She fell to her knees and embraced him. "How did you find us?" she asked. "How did you get here?"

Soon Charles's brothers were crowded around the doorway. Rhoda told Charles that his father was in town looking for work and would not be home until late. The rest of the family ate a simple evening meal together around the oil lamp. Charles felt wonderful being with his mother and brothers again.

That night Charles lay on the floor of the hut with a thin blanket over him. His brothers' bed had no room for him. As he lay there thinking about life, his joy at seeing his mother and brothers turned to anxiety. What would happen when his father came home? Or tomorrow when he wanted to eat breakfast with the others? Would there be enough food for them all?

As if on cue, Charles heard the door creak open, followed by his father's faltering footsteps. He trembled as he felt his father's presence towering over him. He waited for a punch, but instead he heard words. "What are you doing here? You're supposed to be in school. Your grandfather is responsible for you now, not me."

"Kaleli sent me here. He said he can't look after me anymore," Charles whispered back.

"What? Why is that?" his father asked.

Charles did not answer. He didn't really know why himself.

Daudi grunted. Charles remained tense until he heard him collapse onto his own bed.

That could have been a lot worse. At least he didn't hit me, Charles thought as he tried to get back to sleep.

As the days passed, it became obvious to Charles that his father wanted him gone. And the cycle of abuse continued in the home. Getting back to school was constantly on Charles's mind, and he asked his mother a few times if that would be possible. He felt guilty asking because none of his brothers were at school and the school fees were much more expensive in the city than in the rural villages.

It was Charles's mother who broke the news to him that he would have to go back to her family in Kathithyamaa. She was hopeful that his grandmother would be able to take him in once more. Charles doubted it. If his grandmother would not take him in, Rhoda told Charles, she hoped that one of her brothers would take pity on him. They hadn't proven to be supportive before, but perhaps if they were forced to take notice, one of them would rise to the occasion.

Once again Charles boarded a train. This time the train was taking him full circle back to Kathithyamaa, which he had left over two years before. As the train chugged away from Nakuru station, Charles hoped he was headed to a better life, but it was a distant hope. Not much had gone right for him in his life so far, and he couldn't imagine things changing anytime soon. *What would it be like*, he wondered, *to have someone—just one person—who really wanted me?* This was a question he thought about for a long time on the train ride back to his mother's village.

No one was waiting for him to arrive back in Kathithyamaa. Charles walked the familiar route to his grandmother's house alone. Before he got there, he was intercepted by two of his uncles. "Why did you come back? Where are you going?" they asked him.

"To see Grandma," he replied.

They shook their heads. "No, she does not want you back. We don't want you back. You are not our responsibility. Go to your Aunt Muthikwa. She has no children. She might want you."

Charles looked down the path toward his grandmother's house. His uncles stepped closer, blocking the way. It was no use. He turned and retraced his steps. His father's sister Muthikwa lived near the village, but Charles was scared of her husband, Masyuko. Still, by now he had no choice but to throw himself on his aunt's mercy.

Aunt Muthikwa answered the door and smiled when she saw Charles. "Welcome," she said with genuine warmth. "Are you alone?"

Charles nodded.

"Come and tell me how you got here," his aunt said.

From her tone of voice, Charles could tell she really wanted to know. Soon the two of them were drinking hot tea as Charles told his aunt about his family in Nakuru.

Aunt Muthikwa nodded and interjected with a few questions. Although she was his father's sister, the two couldn't have been more different. "Well," she said when Charles was finished, "you can stay with us here. We will make room for you and see about getting you back to school."

Charles was ecstatic. A bed, someone to talk to, and the possibility of going back to school—what more could he want? It felt too good to Charles to be true, and it was. That night Uncle Masyuko came home drunk. "Why is that boy of Daudi's staying in my house?" he demanded.

"He has nowhere else to go," Charles heard his aunt say. He kept his eyes closed, pretending he was asleep. It seemed the safest course of action.

"He's a waste. If they don't want him, I don't either. He'll be a drain on us. Get rid of him now!"

Aunt Muthikwa began to sob. "But the boy is blood. He has no one. If we don't take him in, who will?"

"I don't care. He's not our problem. He's a no-body!" his uncle said as he tugged at Charles's blanket.

Charles then felt his aunt shaking him gently. "Come on, Charles, you'll have to sleep outside," she said.

Charles stood and walked out the door. The stars shone brightly in the crisp night. He heard the door close and then turned to see the silhouette of his aunt beside him. "I am sorry about that, Charles. I will talk to Masyuko tomorrow. Tonight we will both sleep under the stars."

Charles gulped. His aunt had sided with him and defied her husband. It was a risky thing to do, and Charles hoped she did not get beaten for it.

Chapter 4

Making His Own Way

It will get better, you'll see," Aunt Muthikwa told Charles a week after he had arrived. She paid for him to enroll in the local school. Because he had missed so much school, Charles was still in first grade. Rather than feel discouraged, however, he was determined to do what he could to catch up, listening carefully to the teacher and doing everything he was asked to do.

Charles lasted a month at school. The abuse at "home" from Uncle Masyuko became worse by the day, and Charles dreaded the thought that his Aunt Muthikwa might be punished for taking him in. The situation could not go on. Rather than wait to be thrown out of the house, Charles decided to leave and make his own way in the world. He was tired of being a burden to people, tired of being made to feel like a worthless beggar by his own relatives. He would strike out on his own. After all, he told himself, he was a strong eleven-year-old boy—old enough, he hoped, to be hired as a laborer on a farm somewhere. It was difficult saying goodbye to Aunt Muthikwa. Although she begged him to stay, Charles knew that it would never work out. It would be much easier for everyone if he did not bother his family again.

Within a few days Charles found a job in a nearby town digging holes to plant coffee and maize. The work was backbreaking, and he was paid only a few pennies a day, but he didn't mind. He was on his own. He made enough money to pay for his food and a corner of someone's hut to sleep in. He also set some money aside to pay for two hours of schooling each night after his work was done.

Life soon fell into a pattern for Charles. Sometimes he was able to save enough money to allow him to go to school during the day, and bit by bit he worked his way through the second, third, and fourth grades.

On December 12, 1963, when Charles was almost fifteen years old, the teacher announced at school that the day was the most important one they would ever live to see—it was Kenya's Independence Day. That day a Kenyan government elected by Kenyans took control of the country. Kenya was no longer under the rule of Great Britain, as it had been since the late nineteenth century. Charles watched as the red, white, and blue Union Jack (the flag of the United Kingdom) was lowered at the school flagpole and the new black, red, and green flag of Kenya was proudly raised in its place. The teacher explained that of the eight and a half million people living in Kenya, only about fifty-five thousand of them were white. Yet white people owned almost all the property, businesses, and farms in the country. Independence Day signaled a new beginning for Kenya. Native Kenyans would now take their rightful place governing their own country.

Charles hoped that independence would make things better for him, but as the weeks went by, he lost hope of that happening. Every day remained a struggle to survive, to eat enough, and to concentrate on his schoolwork at night.

The period following independence brought turmoil, not peace and prosperity, to the countryside. Now that Kenya was independent and governed by Kenyans, most of the white settlers left the so-called White Highlands and the Rift Valley of central Kenya. Their former plantations and farms were broken up and given to native Kenyan farmers. Since the new government was made up mostly of members of the Kikuyu people, however, they gave the best land to their own tribal people instead of sharing it equally with the Kalenjin and Maasai tribes, who had also lived on that land before the white farmers came. This led to tribal clashes and uprisings. The land redistribution also meant that fewer jobs were available for people in the countryside to earn a living. Thankfully, Charles was still able to find field work.

From time to time Charles would hear snippets of

news about his family. He learned that they had been affected by the changes taking place in the country. In the past his father had been able to make a few pennies here and there doing farm labor, but those opportunities were now greatly diminished. When the new government stepped in and relocated the poorest people from the cities to remote bush areas, it gave the people an opportunity to eke out a living on the land. Charles learned that his family had been moved from Nakuru to Ndalani, an area sixty miles northeast of Nairobi.

Charles tried to be optimistic about his own circumstances. He told himself that things would get better, that there was hope for him. But by the time he was sixteen years old, he had given up hope. He sank into a deep depression and wondered what the point was of struggling so hard to stay alive. His hopes for a brighter future had faded in the drudgery of digging and weeding ten hours a day under the blazing sun. He looked around for other people who might be enjoying their lives more than he was, but all he saw were men who got drunk every night and made life a misery for their families. What was the use of even being alive?

Charles wondered if anyone would even miss him if he died. Slowly he began to form a plan in his mind to take his own life, but before he had a chance to act on his thoughts, a boy who worked alongside him in the coffee fields invited him to a meeting. Charles followed the boy to a large hall in Kathithyamaa, just off the main road. As they approached the steps, Charles heard singing and clapping. He nearly turned back. The last thing he wanted to do was join a party, but something about the music captivated him. Charles followed his friend inside, and together they found a seat in the middle of the hall near an aisle.

Charles soon learned that he had landed in the middle of a youth rally sponsored by the African Brotherhood Church. All around him were young people— about three hundred of them—clapping, laughing, and singing enthusiastically. Charles noticed something warm and inviting about the meeting. After the singing and clapping had died down, the youth took their seats. A middle-aged man clad in a boldly patterned black-and-white shirt stood at the front and began preaching to the crowd. His voice was calm and steady, and to Charles it seemed to fill every corner of the hall.

While Charles had had some religious instruction at school, he had never seen anything like this. He sensed a power and a peace he had never experienced before. He listened carefully to the preacher, and what he heard seemed too good to be true. Was there really a Holy Spirit who would go with him everywhere? Would Jesus be his constant friend? Did God really love him and have a plan for his life? Was there a future and a hope for Charles? Something inside him said, *"Yes!"* He was sure of it. Somehow the preacher was saying things Charles knew to be true. Suddenly his whole world opened up. Someone loved him. Someone would always be with him. Someone would guide him and give him a future. What could be better than that?

When the preacher asked those who wanted to accept Jesus Christ into their hearts to raise their hands, Charles's hand immediately shot up. The preacher asked them to walk to the front. Charles was the first out of his seat. Something felt different, very different. Everything seemed lighter, brighter, more real than before. At the front the preacher asked Charles and the others to repeat a prayer. "God, I need You in my life. I invite You to take control of my life. I ask You to forgive me my sins and help me forgive others who have sinned against me. Take me and make me Your child. Amen."

That was all it took. Charles left the hall that night filled with joy. As he walked past the place where he had intended to end his own life, a surge of gratitude pulsed through him. "Thank You, God," he said aloud. "You saved me from killing myself. Now I will live for You."

Before going to bed, Charles knelt to pray. He wasn't sure what to say, but one phrase kept echoing through his mind. It was something the preacher had prayed: "I ask You to forgive me my sins and help me forgive others who have sinned against me." As Charles closed his eyes, he thought of his father, his useless, abusive father, the man he lived in fear of, who had beaten his mother more times than he could count and who had abandoned him at six years of age. If anyone had sinned against him, it was his father. Was he supposed to forgive someone that monstrous? Charles had hated his father for so long. How could that ever really change? He opened his mouth to pray, but the words would not come out. *I have to pray for them*, Charles told himself. *If God forgives me, I have to forgive others.*

Slowly, painfully over the next few minutes the words began to come. Charles asked God to help him forgive his parents and bless them. As he prayed, he felt incredibly free inside. The hatred that had bound him so tightly was dissolving.

After the first week Charles returned to the hall on Sunday for another meeting. This time he was introduced to the pastor of the African Brotherhood Church and several members of the youth group. They welcomed him warmly. For the first time since leaving his aunt, Charles felt as if someone really wanted to be with him—really cared for him.

Before long Charles was an active member of the church. He went to Bible studies and enrolled in a British Bible correspondence course, which came with a Bible. He couldn't have been happier. He studied at night and wrote Bible verses on scraps of paper so he could keep them in his pocket and memorize them while he worked in the fields. Charles also continued to attend regular school whenever possible. By 1966 when he was seventeen years old, he finished eighth grade—at the top of his class.

Charles was now at a crossroads. He could go on to high school, or he could stop and devote all his time to making enough money to keep himself alive and possibly save a little. Charles felt sure that God had big plans for him and that he should go on to high school and university. He just had to figure out how God would provide the money to do so. High school fees were more expensive than fees for primary school, and Charles knew that he could not earn enough money himself to attend classes. He prayed every night that God would open up a way for him to attend high school. He asked anyone who might help him. Although some of his uncles were doing well in their small businesses, when Charles approached them, he got the same answer: "You are not our responsibility. We have our own families to take care of. Go and ask someone else."

As the start of the new school year rolled around, Charles prayed harder. He wondered if someone at church would sponsor him or if one of his uncles would change his mind. But nothing happened. School started, and Charles watched as the children he had gone to primary school with now walked to high school each morning in their new brown-and-green uniforms. As hard as it was to admit, Charles knew that his dream of going to high school was just that—a dream. The reality was that he would work in the fields while his former schoolmates went on to high school and beyond. Charles realized that one day, five or ten years from now, they could well be his overseers, telling him what to do and doling out his meager wages. The realization stung.

"Where are You, God?" Charles pleaded. "I thought You cared about me and wanted me to have a good life, but You have not provided the money for me to go to school." Charles cried every night for two weeks. Since it made no difference, after that he tried to forget his dream of getting a good education.

Now that he did not have to pay school fees, Charles had a little money left over at the end of each month. He saved it and gradually used it to outfit himself. First he bought a pair of shoes, then a new shirt and pants.

As he worked away in the fields, Charles began thinking about leaving the Kathithyamaa area. As he looked around, he could see no opportunities for him. He wanted to have a wife and children one day, but how could he possibly look after them properly on the wages he was earning? He had to find something else—something better.

In late January 1967, Charles set out for Ndalani, where his family was now living. Since becoming a Christian, he had been praying for his parents every night. He wanted to see them again. As he headed for Ndalani, Charles carried a woven bag with him in which he stowed his Bible and correspondence-course notes, along with some sugar for his mother.

Charles walked all day. The sun was setting as he approached Ndalani, an even more depressing place than he had imagined. The landscape was barren, and a layer of red dust coated everything. There were few gardens and even fewer trees. The huts were made of mud, and emaciated children in rags hung around the doorways. *How,* he wondered, *does the government expect the poorest people from the cities to make a living in a place like this?*

Charles asked around and soon learned where his family's hut was located. It looked as dismal as the other huts. His brother Dickson was sitting outside. He didn't recognize Charles at first, but soon the two of them were hugging. Charles's mother came out of the hut and gasped. "You're back!" she exclaimed. "How well you look."

Charles smiled. His new clothes were a stark contrast to his mother's tattered ones. And his mother looked older and tired, very tired. Rhoda wept as she hugged her son. It felt strange to Charles. For the first time he was taller than his mother. His brothers had also grown. He learned that his mother had given birth to two new brothers.

As Charles walked inside the hut, his stomach tensed. There was nothing there—no food, no beds, no table, no kerosene lamp, no schoolbooks. Charles fought against the waves of disgust that he felt toward his father for not working to provide the basic needs of his family.

When his father came home, Charles wasn't sure how their meeting would go. Daudi did not smile or greet him. In fact, Charles wondered if he even registered that his oldest son had come home.

Because the family hut had no room for him, Charles set to building himself a small mud-brick hut next to the family dwelling. He had no idea how long he would stay in Ndalani. Tradition dictated that the oldest son should help his parents financially, and Charles was determined to be a good son.

After two months, Charles was deeply discouraged. He could not find a regular job that paid him enough to help his family. It was now April, the middle of the rainy season, and Charles checked his money pouch. He had only sixpence left. Unless something changed, he would become a burden to his family and not be the help to them he had wanted to be. He soon realized that he would have to leave, find a job elsewhere, and send back money to help support them.

Charles packed his few belongings into a bag and said goodbye to his family. He had decided to head to Nairobi, sixty miles away, where, perhaps, he could find a decent job. *After all,* Charles told himself, *I can now read and write, skills that might make me good for something other than field work.*

Chapter 5

Opportunity

Charles set out on his walk to the capital city. He estimated it would take him three days to cover the distance. He hoped it wouldn't take any longer, since he had no food with him. He sang hymns along the way and read some psalms to bolster his spirit. He drank water from drainage ditches at the side of the road, and occasionally a shopkeeper would feel sorry for him and give him a sugar candy.

As Charles approached the slums on the eastern edge of Nairobi, the reality of what he was doing hit him. He didn't know a single person in the capital. He was a penniless eighteen-year-old from the country. Not only that, as he walked through the slums, he began to feel depressed. The same squalor in which poor people lived in the countryside was all around him. Women squatted beside fires cooking meager meals while young children dressed in ragged clothes ran around. The stench from so many people living together without proper sanitation made Charles gag. Had all these people also come to Nairobi seeking a better life just as he had? Charles stopped and prayed that God would guide him in the right direction. He had no idea where to head in the big, sprawling city.

The sun was high in the sky as Charles approached the suburb of Kileleshwa, two and a half miles from the center of Nairobi. He was amazed at how everything changed abruptly from the other parts of the city he had passed through. The streets here were tree-lined and swept clean, and large bungalow-style houses sat behind tall fences with wrought-iron gates. The houses were surrounded by neatly clipped lawns and beautiful flower gardens. As Charles walked slowly through these streets, he tried to ignore the gnawing in his stomach, a combination of hunger and nervousness.

Charles stopped in front of a large white house. He peered through the metal bars of the gate at the beautiful house. In a courtyard off to the side he could see an old woman folding laundry from the clothesline and a middle-aged man peeling onions over a bowl. Charles took a deep breath. It was time to step up and see what would happen next. He picked up a stone from the road and used it to knock on the gate. The metallic clanging reverberated across the courtyard, and the man peeling the onions looked up. As Charles smiled through the bars, the man came over. "Hello," he said.

"Hello," Charles replied. "Is the owner in?"

"Why?" the servant asked. "Do you know them?"

Charles smiled again. "No, but I want to ask for work. May I please talk to them."

The servant stood there for what seemed like a long time, eyeing Charles up and down. Then he nodded and turned away. Charles watched as he walked into the house through the side door. A minute went by, then two, then five. Charles began to wonder if the servant had really gone to find the owner. He waited and prayed.

A woman wearing a beautiful embroidered skirt and top emerged from the house. Charles could see that she was Indian. "Young man," she said, giving Charles a bright smile, "what can I do for you?"

"I need work," Charles replied.

"What can you do?" she asked.

"Anything you want."

"And how old are you?"

"Eighteen."

"Can you cut grass and weed the garden?"

"Of course," Charles said, hoping he could tell the flowers from the weeds. Until now he had only worked in vegetable gardens.

"And do laundry?"

"Most certainly," he said, feeling his hopes rise. Surely the woman would not be asking such detailed questions if she wasn't thinking of hiring him.

"I think you will do nicely," the woman said. She unlocked the gate and swung it open. "Welcome to our house. My name is Mrs. D'Souza, and I live here with my husband and two sons, Colin and Eric."

Charles stepped through the gate and into a new world.

"You will live in the servants' quarters and eat your meals there, and I will pay you one American dollar a month. How does that sound?"

Charles could hardly trust himself to speak. How did it sound? Like heaven! A house to live in, a steady supply of meals, and twelve dollars a year as well.

As Charles adjusted to life in Nairobi, he often thanked God for how perfectly the new job fit his needs. He soon learned that Mr. and Mrs. D'Souza were from Goa in India and that they were devout Catholics. They understood Charles's desire to go to church and made sure that he had time off on Sundays to do so. Moreover, they both took the time to talk with him and learn about his background.

Work at the house was hard, whether cutting three acres of grass with a hand sickle or hauling the wet bedding up and over the clothesline, but Charles didn't mind. In fact, compared to his previous life he felt positively carefree.

At the end of the first month, Mrs. D'Souza paid Charles his dollar salary. Charles sent most of it to his family in Ndalani through the post office. What little Charles kept for himself he stashed in a tin box under his bed. Bit by bit, he saved enough to make the biggest purchase of his life: a radio. How wonderful it was to sit on a stool at the back of the servants' quarters and listen to the BBC. From the radio he learned that a music group from England named the Beatles was taking the world by storm with a loud and different kind of music. He also learned that an Englishman named Francis Chichester had arrived back in Plymouth, England, after sailing his yacht single-handedly around the world. Charles tried to imagine what sailing around the world on your own would be like. After all, he had never even seen the ocean. He had only read about it in geography books. He also learned that an American spacecraft called *Surveyor 3* had landed on the moon and sent photographs and television images of the moon's surface back to earth. The moon? Charles could hardly believe it. The radio became a window to a wider world for him, a world Charles wanted to be a part of.

It seemed like every week or so Mrs. D'Souza gave Charles some new responsibility. He was allowed into the house to dust the shelves and was sent to the market to buy supplies. Charles worked hard, and although he was grateful for the opportunity to be a house servant, he never stopped thinking about better opportunities. He took correspondence courses from England in various subjects that interested him and was fascinated whenever he overheard Mr. D'Souza having a conversation with his business partners. Cirion D'Souza was a wealthy man. Charles could see that, but he wanted to know how the man had become wealthy. Was it possible to start with nothing and become rich and important? Charles was sure that it was if he trusted God and worked hard.

After Charles had been working at the house for four months, Mrs. D'Souza sat down beside him one afternoon and said, "You are a very hard-working young man. What do you want to do with your life?"

Charles was shocked. He had tried to tell other people, such as his uncles, what he wanted to do, but no one cared or wanted to listen to him. Now his employer wanted to know. He stumbled over his words, afraid that they would sound too outrageous to a wealthy woman. "I want to study and go to university," he said.

"University? Why university?" she asked.

"Because then I will have opportunities, and I will be able to make something of myself."

"Hmm," Mrs. D'Souza said. "You have passed grade eight, am I right?"

"Yes," Charles replied.

"Then you would still have four years of full-time study at high school and another three or four years at university. You are eighteen, so that means you would be at least twenty-six when you finish, if all goes well. Is it that important to you?"

"Yes," Charles replied. "I want a responsible job and enough money to have a wife and raise a family."

"What if there was another way?" Mrs. D'Souza asked.

"How?" Charles asked. "Every good job needs qualifications, and I don't have any."

"Have you considered that there might be another way to find opportunities?"

Charles sat silently. He didn't mean to be rude, but he had absolutely no idea what she was talking about.

"There are opportunities that do not involve going to university," Mrs. D'Souza went on. "You might want to think about that. You have a bright future ahead of you. Keep trusting God."

That night Charles thought about his conversation with Mrs. D'Souza. Had he been so focused on education that he was missing some other way to get ahead in the world? And if so, what was it?

A month later Mr. D'Souza asked Charles to join him in the backyard to talk. He smiled so broadly that Charles was sure he was going to get a raise. It was a good day.

"How would you like a new job?" Mr. D'Souza asked.

Charles frowned. *Is one of the other servants leaving?* he wondered.

"As you know, I work for Kakuzi Fibreland Ltd. We need a new field clerk. Normally we would want someone who has finished high school, but my wife tells me you are her best worker and very smart. The company is prepared to make an exception for you. The job is in Makuyu, about forty miles from here."

Charles wanted to shake himself. Was this really happening? Were his days as a servant over? A field clerk? Yes, he could see himself doing that. "Thank you," he said. "I promise you I won't let you down. This is just the opportunity I have been looking for."

Charles started his new job a week later on Monday, September 15, 1967. Life soon took on a satisfying routine. In the mornings he would head out into the fields to check off the names of the workers and make sure everyone was working well together. Before long he knew the names of all the twelve hundred employees he was responsible for. Then he set about discovering what they and their families needed so he could advise and help them.

In the afternoons Charles would return to his office

to fill out the paperwork. He was given a small office with a desk and a typewriter. He immediately taught himself the art of typing. When his own work was finished, he made a point of helping out anyone else in the office. That way Charles soon learned all of the administrative jobs in the company and paved his way for promotions. To further improve his chances of promotion, he took a correspondence course in accounting and made it a point to be the first to arrive at work each day and the last to leave. All this made Charles a popular field clerk, and soon his workers were inviting him to their huts for meals. Charles took this as an opportunity to teach them about the Bible and how knowing God had turned his life around.

One morning in March 1968, after working for Kakuzi Fibreland Ltd. for six months, Charles walked along a path between the pineapple plants, greeting the workers and checking off their names. Charles was surprised to see a young woman picking pineapples whom he had not seen before. She was tall and slim, and her movements were graceful as she held the top of the pineapple with one hand and chopped the bottom of it with the other. His pulse quickened when he realized he would have to ask her name so she could be put on the payroll. For some reason he felt strangely shy. "Hello," he said.

The young woman looked up. "Hello," she responded, wiping sweat from her face and then smiling.

Charles smiled back. "I don't remember seeing you before. Are you new?" he asked.

"Yes," she replied. "My name is Esther Ntheny. I'm working in my mother's place. Her name is Grace Kavuli. She is too sick to come to work today."

"Right," Charles said, finding her mother's name to check off the list. "I hope she gets better soon." Charles secretly hoped her mother would stay away from the fields for a while—at least long enough for him to get to know Esther better. There was something about her that was different from any other woman he had met.

When Esther's mother returned to work, the company decided to hire Esther as well. For many days afterward, Charles found reasons to stop and talk to Esther as she worked. He learned that she was fifteen years old, had one brother, and had gone to school for only two years. She had to stop because her parents divorced and her mother needed help earning money to live.

This was all interesting, but Charles soon learned one thing about her that impressed him a great deal: Esther was a Christian. Her mother and grandmother belonged to the Salvation Army, and her grandmother worked at the school for the blind that the church ran. Nothing made Charles happier than hearing this. Soon he and Esther began discussing spiritual matters as well. Their friendship quickly blossomed, and Charles found that talking to Esther was the high point of his day. He felt comfortable enough to confide in her about how his family had repeatedly abandoned him and how he dreamed of being an important person with a large business of his own. Esther, too, dreamed of making something of herself, and soon she found work as a maid for an army colonel in Nairobi.

Charles was glad for Esther, but he knew he would miss their conversations. He didn't realize just how much until she was gone. Esther had become the best friend he had ever had, and he wanted to see her again. Charles wrote a letter inviting Esther to visit him. He was delighted when she showed up at his door on one of her days off. The two of them went for a walk together. And although neither of them said it, Charles was aware that this was a new stage in their relationship. They were no longer just meeting as part of the workday. They had deliberately sought each other out. Things were getting serious.

Over the next year and a half, Esther and Charles managed to see each other about once a month. In the meantime, Charles completed his course in accounting and started a new course in business management.

Their friendship having progressed to courtship, Charles asked Esther to be his wife. She accepted his proposal. Of course, Charles was aware that on his current income from Kakuzi Fibreland there was no way he could financially support a wife as well as his parents and eight brothers. To add to the burden, his mother was expecting another child. Charles began searching for a new employment opportunity that would make use of his new accounting and business skills. He applied for every job he thought he could do. Before long, he landed a position with an Austrian company called Strabag. The company had a contract to build new roads in the area between Lake Victoria and the Ugandan border. The job entailed keeping track of the company's construction supplies. Charles's salary would be twice what he was currently earning at Kakuzi Fibreland. The new job had just one catch. It was located in Eldoret, over two hundred miles northwest of Makuyu.

Once Charles would have thought nothing of moving that far away, but now that he was engaged to be married, it was another matter. Kamba custom dictated that a new wife live with her in-laws for the first few years of marriage. Ndalani, where Charles's parents now lived, was over two hundred miles from Eldoret. After discussing the possibilities with Esther, Charles decided to take the job at Eldoret.

On December 22, 1970, Charles and Esther were married at Esther's grandmother's house. It was a small Christian wedding, and Charles sent money for a bus ticket so his parents could attend. He was twenty-two years old, and Esther was seventeen. Charles gave his new mother-in-law goats and cows as a dowry and advised her on how to use them to provide an income for herself and Esther's younger brother.

Following the wedding, Esther went to live with Charles's parents at Ndalani while Charles started his new job at Strabag in Eldoret. With money he had saved, Charles bought a Ford Cortina, which he drove to visit Esther and his family once a month. Other than that, the newlyweds would have to content themselves with communicating by mail, since neither his parents nor any of their neighbors owned a telephone.

At Ndalani, Charles built a simple mud hut next to his parents' hut for Esther to live in. But she was not alone in the new hut. Following the wedding, Charles's parents had given their youngest child, a one-year-old daughter named Miriam, to Charles and Esther to adopt. Rhoda explained that she'd had no luck with girls and that the gods must be angry with her because her previous three daughters had all died. Charles's sister Katumbi had died of malaria, and twin girls had died soon after birth. Rhoda told them she hoped that giving Miriam to Charles and Esther would save the child from a similar fate.

Esther and Charles took Miriam willingly, and it soon felt as though she were their own child. Esther told Charles she prayed for Miriam and for her young brothers-in-law every day as she washed their ragged clothes and cooked their meals. On Sundays she took them all to Sunday school and church. Soon they were all calling her Mum.

Meanwhile, as he always did, Charles began looking for opportunities to improve himself and his situation at Strabag. He worked eighteen hours a day, seven days a week. As a result, he earned a lot of overtime pay, which he needed, since he had offered to give his parents 60 percent of his income with which to take care of themselves, his eight brothers, Esther, and Miriam. He was soon promoted to assistant manager of supplies and charged with making sure that all the heavy road-building equipment was kept fueled.

During his visits to Ndalani, Charles spent time with Esther praying about their situation. Charles was excited when he learned that Esther was pregnant. They both looked forward to the arrival of their baby and a sibling for Miriam. Charles was also proud of the way his wife stood up for her Christian faith. Esther had told Charles that his mother had brought in a red cloth a witch doctor had given her. Rhoda had instructed Esther to sleep on top of it or she would never have healthy babies. Esther refused to do so. She told Rhoda that the witch doctor had no sway over someone who belonged to Jesus Christ.

It was hard for Charles to leave Esther and Miriam at Ndalani after each visit, especially now that his wife was pregnant. Nevertheless, Charles knew that it was what was expected of him. He was determined to honor his parents and fulfill his role as the oldest son. He had no idea how difficult that would become.

Chapter 6

The Power of Life and Death

"I've been trying to do my best, but I cannot do it anymore," Esther sobbed as she cradled baby Jane in her arms. She and Charles were sitting on a riverbank not far from his parents' hut. "It's your father. You send him money, and he spends it on drink and cigars. He hasn't paid the boys' school fees, and there is not enough food to eat. He beats your mother and the boys too. I have never lived in fear like I do now. What happens if he turns his anger on Miriam or Jane? Are we to stay here and be beaten too?"

Charles looked at his wife and their new baby daughter. He felt glum. He had hoped that giving his family money and bringing his bride home would change his father. But it had not. He was just the same, except now Esther, Miriam, and Jane were caught up in the cycle of violence and abuse. It couldn't go on. Tradition or not, his wife and daughters deserved better than this.

"I will talk to him," Charles said.

What followed was one of the most difficult conversations of Charles's life. At twenty-three years of age, Charles was a successful employee with a wife and two daughters and was the owner of a car. His father, in contrast, could not hold down a job, took no responsibility for his own sons, and spent more time drunk than sober. He was violent and abusive. But he was still the father, and Charles, the son. It was almost unthinkable for a son to tell his father what to do, but Charles had had enough. The tables had turned.

Charles talked to his father as if he were the parent and his father the misbehaving child. "I'm taking Esther, Miriam, and Jane away from here," he said. "You are not providing a safe place for them to live. From now on I will only send you 10 percent of my earnings, and you had better spend most of it on the boys. And one more thing. If I hear that you have beaten Mother one more time, I will personally take you to the clan for judgment."

The last words hung in the air. Charles knew there was no going back on a statement like that. Each clan in Kenya had its own justice system. It was no secret that Daudi Mulli was a violent man. If he went before the clan elders, they would condemn him to be beaten to death. Charles watched his father as the information sank in. He saw his father open his mouth several times as if to argue and then shut it again.

"There is nothing more to say," Charles said as he stood up. "You know what you must do, and you know the consequences."

Charles moved Esther and the two girls safely into a small house in Eldoret. He loved having them right there beside him, and he delighted in watching the two little girls grow and develop.

Other changes took place too. In early 1973 Charles was offered a large pay increase by Strabag. But the offer had one catch: the family would have to move to Yemen in the Middle East so that Charles could help oversee a large construction project there. As Charles thought about the new possibilities, he found his heart pulling him in a different direction. *Maybe it is time for a change*, he told himself. *What if, instead of going to Yemen, we stay in Eldoret and I start my own company?*

The more Charles thought about the idea, the more he liked it. Several opportunities came to mind, and Charles settled on running a *matatu* business. A matatu was a shared taxi that followed a set route. Many workers at Strabag lived in a small settlement about five miles outside town and took a matatu to work and back each day. Sometimes they were late because the matatu was overcrowded or did not show up at the right time.

Charles imagined himself ultimately running a large transportation company with buses as well as a fleet of matatus. But he had to start somewhere. He would be the driver, and he would sell the family car to buy a pickup truck he could convert into a matatu by building seats in the truck bed with a canvas canopy over them. Bit by bit he would add more drivers and more vehicles. He even had a name for his company—Mullyways Enterprises. Charles decided to spell Mully with a *y* instead of an *i* to help him keep his business separate from his family.

Charles was excited about getting started, but when he told Esther he was quitting his job for this new opportunity, she did not share his enthusiasm. In fact, she could hardly believe it. "You are what!" she exclaimed. "You are going to give up a perfectly good job with a foreign company to drive a matatu?"

"Not just a matatu," Charles replied. "God has blessed me—blessed us—so much. Look at what we have. I want us to be at the top of society. I'll work hard. There's no limit to how far we can go. The possibilities are endless!"

Esther grimaced. Charles could see that she didn't understand his passion. "Think of it. Without all of the overtime at Strabag, I'll be able to go to church with you and the children on Sundays and get more involved in everything," he told her.

"Yes, there's that," Esther said flatly.

Despite his wife's lack of enthusiasm, Charles followed his dream. He quit his job, sold the Ford Cortina, bought a Peugeot pickup truck, and converted it into a matatu. He then had "Mullyways" painted on the side of the vehicle in bright-red letters. On April 12, 1973, everything was ready to go.

Within weeks Charles had a steady roster of passengers for his matatu and was driving 450 miles a day to the outlying areas and back into the city. The passengers loved the Christian music that blasted from the speakers as they rode along. They also appreciated the way Charles remembered their names and many personal details about them.

Now that he was self-employed, Charles could dress the way he wanted. There was an American shop in town that sold cowboy boots, hats, and jeans. Charles outfitted himself like an American cowboy. He loved his new Western boots. As he drove around town, everyone recognized him by the distinctive brown leather cowboy hat he always wore.

When he worked for Strabag, Charles had spent much of his time in the office or out in the countryside helping to supervise the construction of new roads. But now that he spent most of his time driving to and from Eldoret and around the city, he became aware of just how many homeless children roamed the streets.

As he observed these homeless children, Charles saw in them the same loneliness and hopelessness he had felt as a child. He longed to do something to help them. Soon he started buying loaves of fresh bread and filling bottles with water to take in the matatu with him. When he had a gap in his schedule, he would find a group of street children and share the bread and clean water with them. At first the children were suspicious of Charles and would snatch the bread from his hands and refuse to look him in the eye. But it was not long before street kids were trailing Charles wherever he went, waving at him and calling greetings.

Charles continued to meet more street children. They loved his cowboy hat and the greeting he made up for them. "Ooaye," he would call as he opened his hands wide and walked slowly toward them. Once Charles had won the children's confidence, he would gather them around and tell them simple Bible stories. Soon, it seemed, everyone in Eldoret knew about the matatu cowboy with the special greeting, loaves of bread, and stories for the street children.

It wasn't long before Charles had made enough money from his new enterprise to buy another matatu and employ one of his passengers to be the driver. He also set Esther up with a small shop where she sold drinks, fruit, snacks, and clothes. Like Mullyways, the shop flourished. In fact, over the next four years, everything Charles and Esther did flourished. By 1977 Charles had four matatus and had negotiated to become the sole distributor of gasoline, oil, and lubricants to all of western Kenya. Now Strabag was buying its supplies from him.

Charles and Esther bought eight acres of prime real estate in Eldoret and had a large house built on the land. It was the first stone house built in the city and soon became the hub of social events for the wealthy upper class. Charles was the wealthiest of them all. It seemed hard to believe that he had been a servant at the D'Souzas' home just ten years before. Charles loved to grow things, and soon the rest of the eight acres were filled with fruits and vegetables that had never been grown in Eldoret before. Charles experimented with passion fruit, different varieties of bananas, and mango and orange trees.

By the time the Mullis were ready to move into the new house, Charles and Esther had four daughters. Charles loved watching their personalities develop. Miriam was quiet and loved to read, Jane and Grace were outgoing and constantly asked questions, while little Ndondo tended to her dolls all day long. Charles was delighted to be able to provide a stable home and a bright future for his wife and children. The oldest two girls attended Race Course Primary School and were on target to go to Uasin Gishu High School and then to university. Charles wanted each of his children to have the opportunities he had been denied.

The only discord in the family came from Daudi Mulli, who was up to his old ways again, but ten times worse. Over the years Charles had bought his father cows, goats, and hens, as well as items for the house. Daudi had sold them all to buy alcohol, but worse still, he had begun to trade off his son's name. Charles had bought some property in Ndalani, and his father pretended to be his agent. He sold Charles's land, not once, but three times, to unsuspecting buyers and then spent the money. Charles was furious. It took hundreds of hours to unravel the legal mess his father had created.

Of course, there were still the beatings. Charles thought that his father had reformed, but one day in June 1978, he received word that his mother and

Aunt Muthikwa were on their way by train to Eldoret. As he waited on the station platform for them to
arrive, he grew tense. Why had his mother and aunt
come together without his father?

When the train hissed to a stop at the station and
his mother climbed down from the carriage, aided by
her sister-in-law, Charles had his answer. His father
had beaten his mother to a pulp once more. It was too
much. Something inside Charles snapped. He was
sure that his father would never change. He helped
his mother and aunt to the car and drove them to his
home in silence. There was nothing to say.

That night Charles sat down at his desk and began
to write. "I would like to request a hearing for my
father, Daudi Mulli. He has been beating my mother
and his children for many years and refuses to stop."
When he had outlined all the accusations against his
father, Charles addressed the letter to the chief of the
Aombe clan of the Kamba tribe. He was done. Let the
tribe deal with his father as they saw fit.

A month later Charles stood in an open field with
his mother, Aunt Muthikwa, and many other aunts,
uncles, and cousins. Sitting to their left was the chief
of the Aombe clan, dressed in a brown patterned
cloth and woven orange hat. Beside him were ten or
twelve young men wearing short leather kilts made
from animal skins and carrying an assortment of
clubs, swords, and sticks.

"Charles Mulli, step forward," the chief said.

Charles did as he was instructed.

"You are the oldest son of Daudi Mulli. What do
you accuse him of?" the chief asked.

Charles felt his stomach turn. At that moment he had the power of life and death over his father. It was a terrible responsibility—more terrible than Charles had imagined it would be. He looked back at his mother and thought of all the times she had been beaten within an inch of her life by Daudi and the times Daudi had promised to change but hadn't. *Enough was enough,* Charles assured himself. *Let the clan decide my father's fate.*

Loudly and clearly Charles began addressing the chief. "This is my father, and for as long as I can remember he has beaten my mother. We have asked him to stop for many years. We have begged him, we have bribed him, we have threatened him, but the beatings go on. I have given him many possessions, but he sells them all to buy alcohol. And when he drinks, he becomes violent."

"With just your mother, or with all of you?" queried the chief.

"With all of us. But it is my mother's safety that concerns me today. I do not know how many more beatings she can survive. She is getting older."

The chief nodded and then asked Charles, "You understand how this works? We will listen to testimony and ask your father what he has to say for himself. If we find him guilty, he will be tied down with ropes and beaten until he is crippled or dead."

Charles nodded as his eyes met his father's. They were filled with fear and hatred.

"You will provide a bull to be slaughtered as payment for our services. The clan will cook the bull and feast when this is over. Do you agree?"

"I agree," Charles replied.

"All right then. We will proceed. You say your father has beaten your mother for many years. Is your mother here?"

"Yes," Charles said.

"Tell us why you want this man punished," the chief instructed Rhoda.

Rhoda Mulli stepped forward, her shoulders hunched, her eyes down. Charles could not imagine what was going through her mind. Was she relieved that this was nearly over? Did she feel guilty for testifying against her own husband?

Everyone stood quietly as Rhoda explained the years of abuse that she and her children had faced at the hands of Daudi. She stopped several times to sob or wipe her nose. It was hard for Charles to hear her account. When she finished, she stepped back. Aunt Muthikwa put her arm around Rhoda. Charles was glad that Esther had decided not to come today. The testimony had been gut-wrenching.

"Charles, do you have anything to add to your mother's accusations?"

"I am done," Charles said. "This man has caused so much pain to my mother and our family. We have begged him to change, but he will not. Other people have told him to change, but he threatens to kill them if they interfere. I ask for the clan to intervene once and for all."

The chief then turned to Daudi Mulli and asked, "Is what they say true?"

Charles watched as his father dropped his head and wailed. "It is true," he said. "I have been that man."

"Very well," the chief said. "You shall be punished." He nodded to six strong young men, who grabbed Daudi and threw him to the ground. Daudi screamed. The men pulled off his shirt, tied his wrists and ankles, and then dragged him a few feet away.

The crowd gathered in a circle. This is what they had come to see. A cheer went up as the young men stood around Daudi.

Charles stood wishing it were already over. He could see his father tied facedown on the ground, flailing about. When the first lash came down on Daudi's back, Daudi let out a piercing scream.

Watching his father endure the same agony he had inflicted on his wife, on Charles, and on Charles's brothers for so long brought no satisfaction to Charles. In fact, it had the opposite effect. Charles looked around at the crowd. They were thirsty for blood—his father's blood. Charles was sure that he was the only Christian there, the only one who knew that Daudi was on his way to hell, and the only one who understood the mercy God extends to all people.

"Charles, do something. Help me. I am sorry." His father's voice cut through his thoughts.

"Kill him. Kill him," the crowd chanted as more lashes and blows cracked across Daudi's back.

Charles tried to block out the sound. He didn't feel liberated. It didn't seem like he was being freed from a great weight. In fact, the thought of having the death of his father on his hands was unbearable. Time seemed to stop as Charles debated with himself. Yes, his father deserved to die, but wasn't God a God of mercy? But what about his mother? If he intervened, wouldn't his father beat his mother again and perhaps kill her? Was it fair to exchange his worthless life for hers?

"Charles, please!" his father yelled.

Suddenly Charles raised his hands. "Stop!" he shouted, loud enough to be heard over the chanting. Silence fell over the group, and every eye turned to Charles. "I want you to stop the beating. I want to plead for my father's life," he said.

The crowd swayed with disappointment.

"What did you say?" the chief asked.

Charles repeated himself.

"Are you sure?" the chief inquired. "You are the one who asked for this. Are you backing down now?"

"I will never do it again. Please save me," Daudi pleaded.

"Yes, I am sure," Charles said.

The crowd grew restless. They had come to watch a beating and death, not a negotiation.

"Very well," the chief replied. "This has never happened before. Daudi deserves to die, but if you agree to pay a fine of one cow, I will order them to stop."

"Thank you," Charles replied.

"And the bull will still be slaughtered, and we will feast tonight," the chief said to the crowd. "But you can go now. There is nothing more to see here." He paused and looked at Daudi. "And as for you, your life has been spared through the compassion of your son. But he has the right to recall you to this court. If you ever come back again, I will not hesitate to have you beaten. And next time, no one will stop it until you are dead. Do you understand me?"

"Yes," Daudi said.

Charles walked over to his father, bent down and untied the knots, and said, "You are a free man. I bear no grudge against you, and I am not going to disown you, but you have to change. You have to stop beating your wife. You have to stop drinking. You have to stop using my name to sell my properties. Do you understand?"

"Yes," Daudi said. "I will change. I never want to come back here again."

"Neither do I," Charles said as he walked away.

Chapter 7

Stronger than the Witch Doctor

Six months later, things were going better than ever for the Mulli family. Charles continued to send money to his parents through the post office bank, and he heard good reports that his father had stopped drinking. The future looked bright and predictable. That is, until the day before Christmas when Charles received a letter from Aunt Muthikwa.

Muthikwa had gone to visit Charles's mother and father and wrote that Daudi had gone back to his drinking. However, Daudi realized that he was risking death every time he drank and begged Muthikwa to help him find a solution to his powerlessness over alcohol. She said they went together to see a witch doctor, who told them Daudi was being haunted by the evil spirits of his ancestors. Even more alarming to his aunt was the pronouncement that not only Daudi but also the entire family were in danger of ruin. Muthikwa begged Charles to come to Ndalani and go with his father to visit the most powerful witch doctor in the area.

Charles felt a heavy weight of discouragement come over him. He had been praying for his father for thirteen years. Would Daudi ever change? Even knowing that the clan chief had said he would be killed if he continued to drink had not been enough of a threat. Charles wondered what he should do.

That night he and Esther discussed their options. They could send Daudi back to the chief to be put to death, they could cut off all contact with Daudi and Rhoda, or Charles could go to Ndalani and accompany his father to see the witch doctor.

"I think you should go," Esther encouraged her husband. "Remember that Jesus said in the Gospel of Matthew, 'All authority has been given to Me in heaven and on earth.'"

"Yes," Charles said. "I don't believe my father understands how powerful God is compared to a witch doctor. Perhaps it's time for him to see for himself."

The following weekend, Charles drove to Ndalani. Along the way he prayed that God would guide his steps and that his father would come to see the futility of what the witch doctor had to offer.

When Charles arrived, Daudi seemed glad to see his son. "We have to get help," he told Charles.

"I agree. But why do you think the witch doctor will help you?" Charles asked.

"There's no one else!" Daudi exclaimed. "Everyone knows that only the witch doctor has the power over the spirits of the ancestors."

"I don't agree," Charles said. "I believe that help comes from the living God. But we shall see. I will go with you tomorrow and see what kind of power your witch doctor really has."

Early the next morning, Charles got up before everyone else. He walked silently to a nearby field and knelt to pray. "God, I know You're the one who is all-powerful. You are stronger, far, far stronger than the witch doctor. You know the problem my father has, and I know that only You have the power to change him from the inside out. Please reveal Your power to him today."

After breakfast, father and son set out to walk to the witch doctor's compound several miles away. They could have taken Charles's car, but Charles didn't want to draw attention to himself and his father. It would be better if they arrived on foot like everyone else. They reached the witch doctor's compound later in the day. Hundreds of people were already seated in small groups on the hillside beside the compound.

As the two men walked through the crowd, Charles noticed many needy people, blind, crippled, and very sick. The people spoke in languages from all over Kenya, and even in a few languages that Charles did not recognize. In fact, Charles realized he had never before been in such a mixed group of people. Asians, Arabs, and Europeans, as well as Africans, were present.

Charles and his father asked a woman how you got to actually see the witch doctor, since such a big crowd was waiting. She shrugged. "Just find somewhere to sit," she said. "See over there. Those people have been waiting for two days. Others are invited in sooner to see him. You have to wait until someone comes and picks you out of the crowd."

Charles sighed. He could see that it was going to be a very long day. He and his father found a spot of ground and sat down to wait. To Charles's surprise, within minutes the witch doctor's assistant stood in front of him and Daudi. "It is your turn. Come with me," he said.

"Really? So soon?" Charles asked.

"Yes, the witch doctor has asked for you."

Charles and his father stood and followed the witch doctor's assistant to a small mud hut with a thatched roof and no windows. As they stepped inside, smoke stung Charles's eyes. Charles squinted to see. A leopard skin lay on the floor, and a man about his age sat motionless in the corner.

"Sit down," the assistant said before backing out the door.

Charles and Daudi each sat on one of the three-legged stools beside the smoky fire. Opposite them, the witch doctor hardly moved. Charles prayed under his breath as Daudi sat expectantly. But it was Charles whom the witch doctor focused on, fixing a cold stare on him. Charles held his gaze. Seconds passed. Then the witch doctor started to shake. First his hands beat against his stomach, then his teeth started to chatter, and he gasped for breath. "Why are you here?" he asked, still staring at Charles. "Why have you come? Why would you do this to me? How can you?"

Then, still shaking uncontrollably, the witch doctor turned to Daudi. "Your son has no problems. Go away and come back the day after tomorrow."

"No," Charles said. "I want you to tell us how you will help my father."

"Leave now," the witch doctor pleaded. "You must go." He started to wail.

The assistant came in. He looked shocked. "The witch doctor is not well. Please go," he said.

Charles grabbed Daudi's arm, and the two men walked back into the sunny afternoon.

After a few minutes of walking in silence, Charles said, "Now do you understand that the witch doctor has no power?"

His father did not speak, and Charles knew that he would not be convinced until the witch doctor spoke directly to him. "You will see," he said. "We will come back in two days like he asked. When this is all over, you will have no doubt that the Christian God is the one with the power."

Two days later Charles and his father returned to the witch doctor's compound. The scene was much the same as it had been on their previous visit. They found a spot to sit. Although it was a few hundred yards from the witch doctor's hut, Charles could see the hut clearly. All morning he watched men, women, and children entering and leaving the hut. Shortly after noon, Charles stood up to stretch. Just as he was about to sit down again, he felt the strangest sensation. It was as if he were watching a movie and the sound had gone mute. Everything around him seemed to turn in slow motion. He could see people talking around them, but he could not hear them. Then out of the corner of his eye he saw a massive flash of light as the witch doctor's hut exploded in a ball of fire.

The people closest to the compound screamed. This time Charles heard them. The fire quickly spread across the dry grass on the hillside. Charles pulled Daudi to his feet, and they ran. Half an hour later they were standing on the opposite hillside staring back at the scene. The entire compound and the hill where everyone had sat waiting to see the witch doctor were charred black. Although the fire was now out, smoke continued to rise from the smoldering embers and spread in long, wispy fingers across the sky. "There's no way the witch doctor could have survived," Charles said as he surveyed the scene.

"You are right," his father replied.

"So?" Charles said.

"So?" Daudi echoed.

Charles could hear the fear and awe in his father's voice. "Can you see that the God I worship is much more powerful than our ancestors and their idols?" he asked.

Daudi did not reply. He just kept walking. Charles knew that his father had a lot to think about.

After returning to Eldoret, Charles began to hear things that made him believe his father really was changing. Aunt Muthikwa wrote to say he had stopped drinking. Rhoda had begun attending a local Christian church, and Daudi did not forbid her to go. Charles continued to pray for his father.

Meanwhile, Charles bought a sixty-two-seat bus so that Mullyways Enterprises could take passengers all the way from Eldoret to Nairobi and back. He had plans to buy several more. Also, his family was growing. On August 17, 1979, Esther gave birth to their first son, whom they named Kaleli after Charles's grandfather. Charles had been praying for a son he could train to follow him into the business. He assumed the girls would follow tribal tradition and marry and move in with their husbands' families one day. But a son would always stay with him and Esther.

Soon after Kaleli's birth, Charles received a letter at his office in Eldoret. It was addressed in his father's childlike handwriting. Charles tore the envelope open and began reading the letter inside. "Son, you have been more of a father to me than I have been to you. You have stood by me when I rejected you. You have helped me when I have harmed you. But I have good news to offer you. I have accepted Jesus Christ."

Charles felt the tears well up in his eyes. "This is amazing. Thank you, Jesus," he whispered as he read on.

"It's hard for me to believe how one decision can change a life, but it has. And I have you to thank. You were right about everything. It's not easy for me to write this. It's hard when I think about who I was.

This is why I want to ask for your forgiveness for what I did to you. I am sorry, Charles. I was wrong."

By now the tears were coursing down Charles's cheeks as he read. His father had finally come to his senses. The nightmare was over. Charles thought about the time he stepped in and spared his father's life, and now his father had repented and turned to God. Charles wondered what would become of him now. It would be fascinating to watch.

That night Charles went home from the office a happy man. "What more could I want?" he asked Esther. "God has been so good to us!"

She agreed. "Everything you touch goes well. The people say Charles lives in the blessings of God."

It was true. In the years since Charles had trekked to Nairobi, penniless and alone, his life had unfolded in a remarkable way. He was now the wealthiest man in Eldoret. Not only that, but also his Christian endeavors had flourished. He was an elder in his church, and his was one of three families who, along with a British missionary, were starting a new church, which was steadily growing. Then there was his family. Nothing made Charles more proud than his beautiful wife, Esther, and their five children. They all loved learning, and he was glad to be able to give them all the advantages he had never had.

Things just kept getting better. The next time he, Esther, and the family visited Ndalani, Charles marveled at how much his father had changed. Daudi stayed at home now instead of leaving every morning to get drunk in the village. He read his Bible every morning and prayed with Charles's mother, who had become a Christian not long before her husband. For the first time, Charles's children were not afraid of their grandfather. Daudi radiated a calm, loving presence so different from anything Charles had ever seen in him before. And the knot that Charles had always felt in his stomach when he was about to see his mother was gone. He knew he would never have to see her bruised, battered, and bleeding from another one of his father's beatings.

Charles bought his parents a cow, knowing that this time they would take care of it. He was confident that his father would not sell the animal and use the money to buy alcohol, as he had previously.

Back in Eldoret, the small church Charles and Esther were helping to start continued to grow until over nine hundred people were coming to the service on Sunday mornings. Charles's daughters sang in the choir, and Charles preached most Sundays. Even Daniel arap Moi, Kenya's president, came to visit him at church, having heard about the great things happening there.

Every day Charles thanked God for his blessings. As far as he could tell, the more he honored God in his daily life, the more God blessed him with wealth. Then something happened to change all of that.

The Challenge

It was mid-morning when Charles pulled onto Kenyatta Avenue, one of Nairobi's main streets. He was in a good mood. The drive from Eldoret had been fast, and he had passed his time thinking about his children and the next steps for all of them. It was 1986, and Miriam and Jane were attending Kessup Girls High School, a Christian boarding school twenty miles northeast of Eldoret. Grace, who was academically brilliant, was on track to be accepted into Alliance Girls High School, the most prestigious girls school in the country. She was interested in business and showed promise in music. In fact, all of the children were musical. Charles and Esther had worked with them from the time they could talk, and now they all sang together. The Mulli children had been featured several times on the national variety television show *Youth of Today*, and reporters had come to the house to film them for a feature story on exceptional children.

While their older sisters either attended or were about to attend high school, nine-year-old Ndondo and seven-year-old Kaleli went to Uasin Gishu Primary School. Charles could hardly believe where the years had gone. He and Esther had had three more children since Kaleli: a now four-year-old daughter, Mueni, and two more sons, two-year-old Isaac and newly born Dickson. Charles chuckled to himself. With eight children, he and Esther had their hands full, but in the best possible way.

During the drive Charles's mind had drifted to the next family vacation. He thought they should all return to Germany. They had vacationed there before, as Charles visited friends he had made while working for Strabag. He loved Germany, with its fast cars and beautiful castles. Charles had also visited a number of other countries—England, France, Canada, and Israel. Some of the trips were for pleasure, and others were for business as he bought engine components and accessories or negotiated oil deals.

Charles watched for a parking space as he drove down Kenyatta Avenue. There were none. He drove slowly through the parking lot next to Nyayo House, the building where he needed to go. Still no parking space. Suddenly a group of seven or eight older street kids stepped in front of his car and beckoned for him to follow them. Charles edged the Peugeot forward as the boys guided him toward an empty parking space.

That wasn't so hard, Charles thought as he grabbed his bag and locked the car door behind him.

"A shilling. Give us a shilling for helping you," one of the older boys said, thrusting his hand toward Charles.

Charles hesitated. Normally he had no problem giving street children food or money, but he had caught the strong smell of glue coming from the boys. Two or three of them looked as though they were high. If he gave them money, Charles was sure they would use it to buy more glue to sniff. He shook his head and looked around for a kiosk where he could buy them some food. He couldn't see one.

"Give us a shilling," the boy said again. "We'll watch the car for you and make sure nothing happens to it."

Charles came to Nairobi at least once a week, and nothing had ever happened to his car. "No, it's okay," he said, walking past the boys.

The boys followed him, begging for a shilling, but Charles could not bear to think of supporting their glue sniffing. He walked faster until he reached Nyayo House, where he passed the security guards and disappeared behind the building's thick glass doors. He was thankful to be inside the government building, where he had come to renew the licenses on his six buses.

The process of renewing the licenses went smoothly, and a half hour later Charles was ready to go home. He walked to where he had left the car, but the space was empty. Thinking he might be mistaken, he doubled back, looking for his gray Peugeot, but he couldn't see it.

One of the street boys sauntered by. "Have you seen my car?" Charles asked.

The boy shrugged his shoulders. "Did you ask me to watch it?" he said.

Charles took a deep breath. He had to face it. His car had been stolen, and the group of street boys either knew who took it or had stolen it themselves. There was nothing else he could do but go to the police station and report his car missing. Charles could have called for one of his workers to come to Nairobi and pick him up, but he decided to take a bus home, a Mullyways bus that drove from Eldoret to Nairobi and back each day.

It was an odd experience for Charles, now a multimillionaire, to be sitting on his own bus as an anonymous passenger for the 180-mile trip back to Eldoret. He watched as passengers stowed their belongings and their purchases in Nairobi for the trip. Some people were busy in conversation. Others napped or read the newspaper.

As the bus rolled along, Charles's mind drifted back to the incident of his stolen car. The fact that it had been stolen didn't bother him too much. He owned twenty buses and cars by now, and something was always happening to one of them. The Peugeot was insured and would be easy to replace. It was the street boys that Charles couldn't stop thinking about. He wondered how they had come to live on the streets in the first place. Did they have parents? Had they ever been to school? How many of them were addicted to sniffing glue or drinking cheap alcohol? And whose fault was it that the boys were like that? The government's? Their parents'? Society's? Charles thought about this for a long time until he realized that it didn't matter whose fault it was. He knew the real questions: Who is going to fix it? Who is going to help those boys find a better life? The questions lodged in his heart and would not leave.

No matter what Charles did, the image of those street boys in Nairobi kept coming back, and the question *Who will help them?* haunted him. Three months went by, and then six. Charles spent sleepless nights thinking about the boys, wondering where they slept, whether they were safe, and whether they were hungry. He knew they were most certainly hungry. By now Charles was giving out more bread and milk to local street kids in Eldoret than ever before. He also gave money to his nieces and nephews so that they could attend school, and he gave generously to his church and many other organizations.

Soon another question began to weigh on Charles regarding the street children: Am I doing enough? True, he was doing far more for them than just about anyone else he knew, but was it enough? He wondered if that was all God required of him, or was he missing something? Perhaps there was some new ministry he should add to his life.

Three years after his car was stolen in Nairobi, Charles was still thinking about the street boys and their situation. Then one Monday in November 1989,

Charles started to feel sick at work. He quickly took care of the most important matters and told his secretary he was going home to rest. Charles got into his Mercedes-Benz and pulled out of the parking lot.

The next thing Charles knew, he was driving down an unfamiliar road. He wasn't sure where he was. He studied the next road sign that came up. It read "Turbo." Turbo? That was twenty miles from home on the way to Uganda! Charles didn't know what had happened to him. How did he get here? He decided that he must have blacked out while still being able to drive. He thought of all the intersections he must have driven through, all the cars he must have passed. How did he stay on the correct side of the road? Charles was amazed that he hadn't been killed.

Overwhelmed, Charles pulled off the road. As the car came to a halt, he began to cry like a baby. What if he had been killed? Would he have already done everything God had wanted him to do? What would his legacy be? Sure, he told himself, he was a good Christian man, he was very active in his church, and he gave away far more than 10 percent of his income. He now had eight children to support and nurture who were all doing well; his marriage was happy and stable; his parents were now Christians, as were most of his brothers. But as he continued to cry, the same question he had wrestled with for three years remained. Who would help the street kids? No matter how he had tried to ignore that question, it challenged him.

Charles sat in his car praying, crying, and begging God for a clear answer about what he should do next. He felt sure that he was not doing enough. He came to the conclusion that either he had to forget about the street kids or he had to commit his life and resources to helping them. Charles wrestled with the decision before him. He took great pride in providing well for his family. What would happen to them if he chose to help street kids? And was it fair to Esther to ask her to give up so much? They had eight children. Wouldn't now be the worst possible time to put everything they knew and had in jeopardy? Charles didn't have answers, but he was determined not to drive home until he did.

For three hours he sat in the car on the side of the road. "God, show me what to do. I will obey what You tell me. I'm ready to move by faith and be used by You," Charles found himself praying. "I'm willing to give up everything You've blessed me with. Use me to reach those kids, Lord. They are just like I was, without hope. Help me bring them hope."

At that moment everything changed. It was as if someone had switched the station on his car radio. Charles felt a flood of peace rush through him. Suddenly it was as if he had nothing to worry about. He knew everything would work out. Esther, the children, his parents—God would take care of it all. "Thank You, Lord," he prayed. "I will be with You on this journey wherever it takes us, and You will be with me. I will serve only You. I will do my best."

Charles laughed out loud and then burst into singing. He had made his decision. His whole heart was in the challenge that lay ahead. As he drove home,

Charles decided to tell the family at dinner about this new direction.

"I have an announcement to make," he said as the family finished eating.

Immediately all eyes were on Charles, as if everyone realized that something very different was about to happen.

Charles cleared his throat. "Our family has been blessed. But being blessed is not the chief aim in life. I can keep working to give you more things, a bigger house, more to put in it, more vacations and clothes and books and sports equipment. But is that what our lives are supposed to be about? Our family serves God, and God is leading us in a new direction. We can either follow Him or go back to what we had before."

He stopped for a moment. The room was electric. No one made a sound. Even little Dickson did not wiggle in his chair.

"As you all know, I've had a burden for street children for years. I was just like those street children before Jesus rescued me. Now I cannot fight my calling any longer. Jesus is asking me to help the street children, this I know for sure. I have made my decision. I cannot stay in business. I am giving it up. I'm selling all our businesses, and I'm going to find a way to help those children. I will never work for money again as long as I live." He looked at Esther, but she was looking down.

Everyone sat around the table still as a statue. No one seemed to want to be the first to break the silence. At last Jane said, "We'll be praying for you, Dad."

Esther spoke next. "That's quite a change," she said in a voice just above a whisper.

"Yes, it is," Charles replied.

More silence.

After dinner the children went to their rooms to do their homework and, Charles suspected, to discuss what lay ahead for them. Yesterday he would have felt bad that he could not tell them what was next, that he could not assure them that they would be able to stay in the top schools and attend the best universities. Now he could offer no guarantees. It was up to God to guide them. Charles smiled to himself as he went to help the two youngest children, Isaac and Dickson, get ready for bed. He could hardly wait for tomorrow.

Later that night, when all the children were in bed, Charles stood in his backyard praying. Soon Esther joined him. He held out his hand to her, but she did not take it.

"Everything?" his wife asked in a flat voice. "You're going to get rid of everything we have worked so hard for?"

Charles nodded. "Yes. God is with us. I know He is. I feel such peace."

Esther grunted. "How can you do this? I don't understand. How can you separate yourself from your house, your money, your family?"

Charles swung around. He could see her face in the moonlight. She looked exhausted. "Esther, this is not separating me from the rest of you. I know I have a responsibility to you all. God will take care of all of us. I want us to go into this together."

"Couldn't you just sell some of our properties and work part-time for the businesses and part-time for the street children? Does it have to be all or nothing?" Esther asked.

"God has spoken to me, and I have faith He will provide," Charles replied. "Are you with me?"

The question hung in the still, night air.

Chapter 9

"What Can I Do for You?"

It was nine o'clock in the morning as Charles flipped his day planner open to Tuesday, November 18, 1989. *This is when it all begins,* he said to himself, picking up his pen. He would normally be in his office at work by now, but he had already called his secretary and asked her to cancel all of his meetings for the day. In the day planner Charles crossed out all the now-canceled appointments. For his morning activity he wrote, "Begin process of divesting myself. Lawyers? Contracts? How many accounts? When to notify employees?" For the afternoon slot he jotted down, "Plan strategy for reaching street children and others. Where to go? What to take? Then GO!"

Charles had never before felt this excited, this energized. He spent the morning making lists of who he would have to contact and what he would have to do to close all his various businesses, including the oil and gas franchise and his real estate management and insurance company, and to dispose of all the buses, cars, trucks, and properties associated with each business. Charles called his lawyer to begin discussing the legal issues surrounding terminating contracts and licenses with companies he had agreements with.

All of that was about dealing with the past. As he looked ahead, Charles eagerly took a blank sheet of paper and titled it "Reaching the Street Children—Strategy to Start." As he stared at the paper, his mind whirled with a million possibilities of how to spend the money from his business ventures: medical clinics for street kids, a police force trained to help kids rather than take advantage of them, food recycling and distribution centers so the children wouldn't go hungry, schools for them, even a new family to give them a sense of belonging and value, and most of all, the opportunity to know God and be transformed by His power.

"Lord," Charles prayed, "You know the way ahead. All I have to do is follow. I ask You to lead me now."

After more prayer, Charles felt he should work at providing food for the street children. "It's hard to concentrate on anything when you're hungry," he told himself aloud. "Then I'll share the gospel with them and take it from there. God has a plan for their housing and education. My job is to get to know the children better and win their confidence."

Early in the afternoon, Charles bounded downstairs. Esther stood in the kitchen preparing vegetables for dinner. Her eyes were red and puffy. Charles felt compassion for her but not regret for what he was doing. "It will be hard, but it will be worth it," he told his wife quietly. "God will not let us down. I know this is the right thing to do."

Esther tipped sweet potatoes into a pan. "That's all right for you. You have this great faith. But what about the rest of us? What are we supposed to do? Our children are scared. Jane asked me this morning if we were still going to send her to university. What are their friends going to say if the children start mixing with street kids? There are so many things you haven't thought about, Charles," Esther continued. "These kids are thieves and gang members. I'm sure some of them have murdered and assaulted people. You know what the streets are like at night. You read the news. Some of them have TB and other contagious diseases. They are glue-sniffing drug addicts with knives. How can you guarantee me you will be safe out there? Do you want me to be a widow? Do you? Does God really want you to put your family at risk like this? What is the point of sending our children to the best schools and then exposing them to the worst children?"

"I can't answer those questions, Esther," Charles said quietly, "but I know I'm doing the right thing. I'm certain this is what I—we—have been called to do, and the way will unfold as we are obedient to God. I am going to buy some bread and milk now and take it to the street kids."

Esther barely turned as she mumbled goodbye.

Charles stopped to buy supplies and then headed to the poor areas of town, where he drove his car up and down the streets until he found groups of street children. Then, as he had done many times before, he approached the children, his palms upturned and calling "Ooaye," the made-up greeting he had been using for many years when approaching street children. When he had the children's trust and attention, he asked, "Would you like something to eat?" As usual, Charles noted the promise of food quickly overcame any reservations the children might have toward him. They gathered around him as he pulled loaves of bread from his car, broke them apart, and handed chunks to the children. They gobbled the bread down and drank the milk he had to offer them.

Often in the past when Charles had offered food to the street children, he had been pressed for time. He had to drive his matatu route or had things to do at the office or family matters to attend to. Today, Charles had lots of time. He introduced himself to the children and listened to what they had to say.

After a group of street children had gathered, Charles led them to the church he had helped to establish and where he often preached. The children sat on the field next to the church and ate bread and listened as he told them stories from the Bible and explained to them about Jesus—who He was and that He loved each of them, just as He loved Charles.

After telling the children several Bible stories, Charles looked directly at the group. "What can I do for you?" he asked. The street children fell silent and stared at him. Inside he chuckled. He would have had exactly the same reaction had someone asked him that question when he was a child struggling to survive. But no one ever cared that much about him back then to ask the question. And he was sure it was the first time anyone had ever asked it of these children.

"What can you do for *us*?" one boy finally asked, incredulous.

"Well," Charles said, "I will bring you bread again tomorrow, and we can talk some more about the Bible and Jesus and your lives. But what else do you need? What else can I help you with?"

The children began to speak up and describe their needs. After food, their two most pressing needs appeared to be a safe place to sleep at night and clothes to wear.

"All right. It might take some time, but I will try to come up with a way to meet your needs."

As he drove home that evening, Charles was invigorated. He recalled each of the children by name and prayed for them all. He thought about their most pressing needs. Clothes wouldn't be too difficult to start with. Everyone in the Mulli household had far more clothes than he or she could wear in a week. Charles decided that he would go through his own wardrobe at home and ask the children to go through theirs to see what clothes they could part with. A safe place to sleep was a little more challenging. Charles thought about an unused shed that stood at the back of the church property. Perhaps it could be cleaned up and the children could sleep inside it.

The next day Charles followed the same pattern as the day before. In the morning he worked on dissolving his companies and then headed out in the afternoon to see the street children. And they were waiting for him, responding to his "Ooaye" and greeting him with smiles. Several other children joined the group as they sat around Charles's car eating bread and drinking milk and sodas. When their stomachs were full, Charles once more invited them to follow him to the church, where he told them more Bible stories and organized a game of soccer. At first the soccer game was chaotic. The children had never been asked to follow rules before, but they caught on to the importance of the rules and were soon enjoying themselves. As Charles refereed the game, he felt an immense sense of pride, almost as if they were his own biological children playing well together.

Bit by bit Charles helped the street children improve their lives. Together they cleaned out the old shed at the church, and the boys began sleeping there at night. The church also had an acre of unused land, which Charles was given permission to use. He organized the children to dig up the weeds and start a vegetable garden. He hoped to use the garden to train street children how to productively farm small blocks of land and to learn the value of practical work.

On the second Sunday after beginning to spend time daily with the street children, Charles invited them to come to church. About twenty showed up, but things didn't go as Charles had hoped they would. One of the elders took him aside and said, "What are these children doing here? They stink and they will contaminate the seats. You have to tell them to go now or we won't have anyone left in the congregation. You need to think seriously about what you are trying to do, Charles. This is not the place for those children."

Charles went back to the children who were occupying the back two rows of seats. "Come on, kids," he told them. "The church is going to be very full today and needs some of the children to have a service outside under the trees to make room for more adults inside."

The street children followed Charles outside, where they all sat down under a jacaranda tree, not realizing that they had been kicked out of church. Charles preached to them and taught them two new songs.

That night Charles prayed for a long time. He was deeply disappointed that the people in the church— his friends and fellow Christians—had been so rude to the street children. He knew that the children were a challenge, but he had hoped that the church would partner with him to reach the children and bring them to Christ. Now he wondered if the church members might end up being a stumbling block for the children. He certainly hoped not.

After two weeks with the street kids, Charles asked Esther if she would cook something for them, since they needed more nutritious food. Esther agreed, and the next day she accompanied Charles to the church with large pots filled with chicken stew and beans. The children ate hungrily. As Charles watched, he was sure it was the first time some of them had eaten a meal cooked just for them.

At home that night Charles asked Esther, "So what did you think of the children?"

She let out a deep sigh. "They need help. Anyone can see that. They are filthy and smelly and hungry. How does anyone live like that with no one to love them and no one to care?"

"God has called us to do that for them, Esther," Charles replied gently. "Are you with me?"

Esther was silent for a long time. "Yes, Charles, I am with you," she replied.

Tears filled Charles's eyes. "Thank you," he said. With his wife working beside him, there was nothing they could not do.

The next two months were challenging. Thirty children showed up at the church each day for food, activities, and Bible stories. As they became more comfortable with Charles and Esther, they began telling them terrible stories about the ways they had been abused on the streets and some of the things they had to do to get enough food to eat. Many of the children were scared and had joined gangs to try to protect themselves from being attacked and assaulted. But sometimes the older gang members assaulted the younger ones, who consequently were not safe anywhere.

This reality made Charles and Esther sad, and they determined to do all they could to bring God's love into the children's lives.

"We can't leave Susan and David on the streets," Esther told Charles one day. "Susan is six and David is three. Every time I say goodbye to them, they follow me like lost puppies. I can't look back at them, and I wonder if we will see them again. I've asked around, and their mother has just disappeared."

Charles nodded. He knew what his wife was feeling. "They can't sleep in the shed with the big boys. What should we do?" he inquired.

"Bring them home?" Esther suggested.

Charles hugged her. That was exactly what he had hoped she would say.

"Can we do that?" Esther continued. "I mean, do we have to tell anyone we're taking the kids?"

"I'll ask around, but I don't think there are any legal requirements," Charles said. "That's why it's so dangerous for them all out there. They have no one to watch over them. And there's Jane Washuka. She's only four. I know her mother has died. Shall we bring her home too?"

"I suppose so. We'll have quite a house full!" Esther said with a chuckle.

Several days later the three new children moved into Miriam and Jane's bedroom. At the time, the two Mulli girls were away at university and boarding school.

The first night, Charles and Esther dressed the three new arrivals for bed in Mueni's and Isaac's pajamas. The next morning the bedroom reeked. All three children had wet their beds. "I'll have to get plastic mattress covers," Esther told Charles. "I thought I was over toilet training when Dickson got out of diapers."

The new children were a challenge to train. When they ate, they would pick the meat from chicken bones and then throw the picked-over bones over their shoulders onto the kitchen floor. It appeared the street children had no idea of the purpose of a plate. Neither did they seem to understand about owning things. Toys, articles of clothing, and other items that Charles and Esther supplied the children with were soon lost. The children had laid them down and had no idea where they left them.

The children had no idea about personal hygiene, either. They had never held a toothbrush or had a shower or sat on a toilet. The bathroom soon looked like a war zone, and somehow one of the children even managed to break the toilet bowl in two.

"It's difficult," Esther told Charles soon after the street children moved in.

"Very difficult," Charles agreed.

"They are so untrained. Our own children are complaining. We're not one big happy family. They resent the new kids, and who can blame them? The street kids have no idea how to behave in a house. And I haven't had a friend visit in a month..." Esther's voice trailed off.

It was true. As the family had grown bigger with the addition of the street children, Charles, Esther, and their children began noticing their friends disappearing fast. It was subtle at first. The Mulli children received fewer invitations to play at their friends' houses. When Esther volunteered to help plan a big party at church, she was told they already had enough people. The older children were moody because their friends had heard rumors that Charles wanted to give everything the family owned to the poor. Even at church, not as many people stopped to shake hands and chat, and the pastor always seemed to be busy when Charles dropped in for a talk.

Still, nothing prepared Charles for what happened one day in mid-September. That day he had gone about his new daily routine, spending time in prayer at home before going out into the streets to help the children. In the afternoon the children and Charles went as usual to the church grounds for a meeting.

Late in the afternoon, about eighty street children sang a number of Christian choruses as their time together with Charles began to wind down. Although the children were still involved in street life, Charles could detect real changes taking place in the lives of some of them. They were asking questions about what was right and wrong and how to stop being violent or stealing. Charles was heartened. He knew they had a long way to go, but these signs were encouraging.

As the final bars of the chorus the children had been singing faded away, Charles noticed two cars pull up in the church parking lot. *That's odd*, he thought. *I didn't think there was anything going on at church tonight.* Two elders, one a university lecturer and the other a businessman, walked toward the building. Charles waved, but they did not respond. Soon more cars pulled up, and more men in suits and ties got out. It looked like a meeting of the entire church board was about to take place, except that Charles, a member of the board, had not been invited. Charles was puzzled. How could they have forgotten to invite him?

After dismissing the street children, Charles strolled into the meeting room with a big smile on his face. His presence was met with stony silence. No one looked him in the eye. In fact, many of the board members stared down at their folded arms. *What on earth has happened?* Charles wondered.

"This has to stop," he heard Joseph, a fellow elder, say.

Charles was indeed puzzled.

Chapter 10

Family

"What do you mean? What has to stop?" Charles asked.

"The street kids, of course. You have to stop bringing them here. You have to stop letting them sleep in the shed at night. You have to stop bringing them to church on Sunday. All of it. It has to stop," another elder said.

Charles felt as if he had been punched in the stomach. "Why?"

"You know why as well as we do," Joseph said. "It's too much. They don't belong here. They are useless, and nothing good will ever come of them. They have lice, and they stink with infections. But that's not the worst part. Charles, you must be practical. They are gang members and thieves. They don't belong

111

with our children in our church. I imagine you will want them to join the youth group soon. It's just not going to work. Everyone has put too much into this church to watch it be destroyed by your crazy scheme."

"No one has put more into this church than me," Charles said quietly. "You all know that Esther and I were among the three families that founded it, and now we are nineteen hundred strong. I love this church, and I believe we are on the right track. I don't want to go on alone. I want you to join with me in helping the street children. We can teach them the Word of God together and educate them so they can get off the streets. I know for sure that God is going to do amazing things with them. Please believe with me."

The room was silent. Then Joseph shifted in his chair and cleared his throat. "It's too late, Charles. We have already met without you and taken a vote. You only have one vote, so even if we let you talk, anything you say won't make a scrap of difference. We have already decided. The street children cannot come back here. You have to get rid of them before they bring our own children down to their level. This is a holy place, and those children are certainly not holy."

Charles looked around the room from person to person. They were friends, prayer partners, fellow Sunday school teachers, and not one of them returned his gaze. He knew that he had lost. The elders' minds were made up. There was no point in staying. "I am sorry you all feel that way. The gospel is powerful enough to transform these street children. What does it say about the way our children are being raised that we cannot trust them to God as well? But I see you have made up your minds." With that Charles stood and walked toward the door. No one called out to stop him.

Charles drove home, stunned at this new development. One thing he knew for sure: he was not going to give up on the street children. If the church did not want them, he would build extra rooms at his house and welcome them there.

When he arrived home, Charles told Esther what had happened. "I am not surprised," she said flatly. "None of my church friends visit or call me anymore, and the other night when I dropped Ndondo off at youth group, the leader didn't even say hello to me."

"Just as well. God is bigger than the church," Charles replied. "If they don't want the poor and the needy, we will make room for them here."

"How?" Esther asked. "We already have three new children, and that's been wild. Today Susan flushed her blouse down the toilet. I don't know why. David and Dickson got into a fistfight. And our kids are miserable. They don't dare complain to you, but they constantly complain and cry to me. The new kids steal their school supplies and their clothes. We're going to have our own wars right here in this house if something doesn't happen. It's just not possible for everyone to get along. They are all too different. We haven't brought our children up that way."

"We certainly need a lot of grace, don't we? But it will work out. I know this is what we're called to do," Charles said. "I'll draw up plans to add another wing onto the house and expand the kitchen. We'll need another oven, don't you think? And I'll work with the bigger kids and teach them how to construct their own sleeping huts in the backyard."

Esther's shoulders slumped. "If that's how it has to be. We've already lost all of our friends, and our children are getting teased at school. I suppose we should keep going and see what happens."

"God is with us!" Charles said. He felt invigorated despite the meeting at church. "God is humbling us, and that's fine. He's not going to humiliate us though. Just wait and see. This morning I read the verse 'Humble yourself under the mighty hand of God and in due time He will exalt you.' We have to press on, Esther. Too much is at stake."

The following day, Charles invited the children who normally gathered at the church into his yard for food and Bible stories. They hung all over his children's swing set and trampled the flower beds. Charles fixed up the garden hose so that they could take makeshift showers, and Esther fed them beans and rice. In the late afternoon they all sat around and planned where the sleeping huts for the boys were going to be erected. Charles was sure it was the first time most of the children had ever been asked to participate in a decision that affected them. Their eyes shone with anticipation.

Over the next few months, the Mullis' home turned into a haven for street kids, but it came at a price. Nearly all of the china was broken, and many items were pilfered from the house. Esther set up a lice-picking station under a banana tree, and Charles paid for a doctor to visit the children and prescribe medicines for the various skin diseases and infections they had.

The street children soon took all of Charles and Esther's time, and what to do with their own biological children became a serious issue. Charles did not want them falling behind in school, and it was almost impossible for them to study at night with all of the distractions around them. But worse still, his own children were constantly complaining about the street kids. It was never-ending. Charles asked them to be kind and share, but they weren't in the mood for it. The house had divided into two camps—his biological children versus the street kids—and it soon turned into war.

"This isn't good for anyone," Esther told Charles. "Our children—our biological children—are suffering. They can't adjust, and the street kids aren't doing as well as they could be, either. It's just not a good fit to bring them here to share with our children. They need so much teaching and attention. I just don't have the time for everyone, and you are always out finding more children to bring home."

"I understand," Charles replied. "I had hoped that our own children would have behaved better and that we could have pulled together as a family. Now I see that that is not going to happen, at least not yet. We need another answer. We need to pray about it."

A week later Charles was sure that God had given him a solution, which he told Esther about.

"Boarding school?" she asked. "Charles, you really want to send Kaleli and Mueni off to boarding school? They are only eleven and eight years old. How could you even think that's a good idea? They are not big enough."

"I think it's God's solution at this time," Charles replied calmly, "and I want you to pray about it."

"All right," Esther agreed.

It was a very difficult decision, but Esther and Charles decided to put Kaleli and Mueni in boarding school. Ndondo and Grace were already away at boarding school, and by now Miriam and Jane were attending university. This would leave six-year-old Isaac and four-year-old Dickson at home with the street children.

Esther wept as they made the decision. "It is such a sacrifice," she said. "How are you sure it will be worth it, Charles?"

Charles felt tears rolling down his own cheeks. All he had ever wanted was to raise his children and to have them near him, and now he was sending them away. "I know this is what God wants us to do. Jesus said, 'Unless a grain of wheat falls into the earth and dies, it remains alone; but if it dies, it bears much fruit.'" He looked Esther in the eye. "We have to believe that. It is a sacrifice. It does feel like dying, but we have to believe that many, many wonderful things will come of this. Do you believe with me, Esther?"

Esther slowly nodded. "This certainly is a different life from the one we used to lead," she said quietly, "but I'm with you."

Over the next year, many alterations were made to the Mullis' home. The children worked hard and built an extension to the main house. They went on to construct simple huts in the Mullis' yard for classrooms, a kitchen, and an outdoor dining pavilion. The sewage lines were enlarged and connected to the city council's main sewer. Bit by bit, the clipped lawns and colorful flower beds were replaced by paving stones and concrete-block buildings.

By the end of the first year, Charles and Esther had worked out a system for getting legal custody of children. They wrote in a log book the details of where each child was found and any information the children knew about themselves. Charles would then go to the police station to register the children living with him and to make sure that no one was looking for a particular child. No one ever was.

Now that they lived at the Mullis' home, all of the children five and older started school. Since the older children had never been to school before, they all started in first grade. Because the children came from many different tribes, they were taught in Swahili, the official language of Kenya. Many of their birth mothers had moved to Eldoret from other parts of the country to eke out a living.

Each month more children were added to the group living with Charles and Esther. The family was now officially being called Mully Children's Family.

When he named it this, Charles had thought of the Bible verse "God puts the solitary in families," and that was exactly what he wanted to do. It was not a giant orphanage or a reform school. It was a family, and Charles and Esther were Daddy Mulli and Mama Esther. Charles trusted that in time God would soften his biological children's hearts and they would embrace the enlarged family.

Two years later, by the beginning of 1993, all of Charles's personal money had long since been spent, but week by week there was enough money to buy food and clothing for the children and to pay the staff. By now there were sixty-two staff members, including teachers, social workers, nursery workers, administrators, and a guard at the gate.

The children were learning to read and write and were acquiring other practical skills. On top of that, as they watched how Charles, Esther, and the other staff lived out their faith, many of them gave their lives to Christ. They told Charles they desired a fresh start on the inside as well. More than anything else, their decision to become Christians and live their lives for God made Charles feel that the sacrifice he had made for the children was absolutely worthwhile.

Late most afternoons or in the early evening, Charles, accompanied by a small team he had trained, visited the slums of Eldoret. They talked with street children and searched out the most desperate to bring home with them. One evening in May, as Charles walked down a narrow alley in the Huruma slum, he saw six young girls sitting with their backs against a flimsy cardboard wall. The girls sat in silence, the kind of silence that Charles knew came from despair. He motioned to the two social workers with him, and they slowed down.

"Ooaye," Charles called as he got closer. The girls hardly looked up. He squatted down beside them. "I am Charles Mulli," he said, holding out his hand to the girl closest to him. "What is your name?"

The girl lowered her eyes and said, "Rael."

"Well, Rael, it's good to meet you and your friends. How are you?"

Rael shrugged her shoulders.

"Can you tell me why you're here so late at night?" Charles pressed, praying under his breath. He knew from experience that now was the moment when a child either trusted and opened up or pulled away.

Rael looked him in the eye. Charles smiled at her. She opened her mouth. "I . . . my mother lives near here, but I can't go home . . . I ran away. Every night my mother would get drunk on *chang'aa* and beat me and my brothers and sisters. In the end I thought it would be safer on the streets, but it's not. Instead of my mother beating me, now men abuse me," Rael said matter-of-factly.

"I'm sorry to hear that," Charles said. "It is very much like my story, except it was my father who beat me, not my mother. I too left home looking for some- thing better, but I didn't find it until I heard about Jesus Christ. Do you know about Jesus?"

"Who is he?" Rael asked.

"He is the Son of God, and He loves you very much. He totally changed my life and gave me hope." Charles talked on for a while, learning that all of the girls were in basically the same position. They had either left their parents or been abandoned and were now living on the streets. Then he asked Rael, "Have you heard of Mully Children's Family?"

Rael nodded. "Yes. Some of the other girls talk about it. They know someone who went there, I think. They say she's okay and has food to eat."

"Well," Charles said, "I'm the father of the Mully family. How would you all like to join us? We can take you now if you want to go. There is food and school and so many things to do, and I will teach you about Jesus. What do you say?"

The girls looked at each other for support. *Will they come or not?* Charles asked himself.

"All right," Rael said. "It can't be worse than this. I'll come."

"Us too," the others said.

"Wonderful," Charles replied. "I'll take you home and you can meet Mama Esther. You will be able to talk with her about your life and how to make it better."

The six girls piled into Charles's car, and he drove them to his home.

At dinner the next night, Charles spotted Rael. By now she had on clean clothes, after taking the first shower of her life. Clinging to her were two of Charles's smaller children. "Look, Daddy," Rael laughed. "I have found my younger brother and sister. You have already adopted them!"

Charles laughed along with her. It felt good to know that Rael was now part of a loving family and that she had been reunited with two biological siblings.

Like many of the other street children, Rael found it difficult to break free of life on the streets. Charles guessed that she was probably addicted to drugs, and although the social workers tried to help her, one day Rael ran away, back to her old life. The lure of drugs and the freedom to go where she pleased were too much for her to resist. This had happened with other children before, and when it did, Charles always responded the same way—he set out to find the child and bring him or her back to the family.

It was pouring rain when Charles spotted Rael in the Huruma slum. She was walking quickly. He yelled to her, but the steady drumbeat of the rain drowned out his voice. Charles stopped his car and walked over to her. "Rael, stop! It's me, your daddy!"

Rael turned to face him, slumping as she did so. Charles noticed a large bruise on her arm. "It's me, Daddy," he said again. "I've come to take you home."

"What's wrong with you?" Rael yelled. "You don't want me. No one wants me. I'm worthless. Go away. Why are you here?"

She turned to walk away.

"Because I love you, Rael," Charles said. Her body began to shake with sobs. Charles reached out and held her tightly. "Rael, we all miss you. Mama Esther misses you. I miss you. All of your brothers and sisters miss you. Will you come home with me?"

Rael wiped her nose with the back of her arm. "I don't want to be here. This is horrible. I want to go home."

"Well, let's get you into the car then. I bet you're hungry."

Rael nodded. "Thank you for coming, Daddy," she whispered.

Street children kept arriving, and somehow Charles and Esther found room for two hundred of them at their house. But by late 1993 it was obvious they needed a bigger home for everyone. Charles began contemplating a bigger facility for his ever-growing family, but where? He knew exactly the place. Although Charles had sold all his businesses and the property that went with them, he and Esther had kept five hundred acres of undeveloped scrub land at Ndalani, where Charles's parents still lived. The land was located beside the Thika River, and Charles and Esther had planned to retire there one day. Since the property was out in the countryside, there were no immediate neighbors to complain about the noise that two or three hundred children would make at the site.

Charles talked to Esther about using the land to build a second home for the children. She readily agreed. After all, she told him, with so many children to raise, it didn't look like they would ever be retiring. Charles was grateful he had a wife who was 100 percent with him in his vision.

Meanwhile, the Mullis' biological children were growing up. Miriam graduated from university with a bachelor of education degree and came back home to help teach the children. Jane graduated with a degree in nursing and fell in love with a local man named Nicky. The two planned to marry. It was satisfying for Charles to see his children focused on their studies and finding their own place in the world, despite the sacrifices they had made.

As Charles prayed about who should initially be sent to Ndalani, he realized it was an opportunity for the most difficult teenage boys to go there and try something different. He asked two teachers to take charge of the seventeen most challenging boys at Eldoret and take them to live on the property at Ndalani. As well as keeping up with their regular studies, the boys would clear the land for farming and build several simple buildings for the other children to occupy when they moved there. Charles felt that hard physical labor and a sense of purpose would do them all good.

Charles and Esther spent a day together on the property on the Thika River, walking, talking, and praying together. It was a refreshing time for them both. By the end of the day, they were encouraged and full of faith for the things God wanted to accomplish on this land.

On Saturday, August 20, 1994, four hundred people, including all the Mully Children's Family members from Eldoret, Charles's parents, and other relatives and friends, arrived at the Ndalani property for a service to dedicate the land. As Charles looked over the barren red scrubland, he saw the future—a lush, fertile area filled with happy children.

Charles's parents sat proudly in the front row. Daudi Mulli was a changed man, an elder in the local church and someone whom people sought out to mediate arguments. Rhoda, too, had a strong faith and worked tirelessly to help the poor women in the area. Most of Charles's brothers had also become Christians, and several of them planned to work for him at Ndalani once the facility was up and running. Aunt Muthikwa had also given her heart to Christ and sat beaming through the whole dedication service.

Afterward, the entire Mully Children's Family traveled to Nairobi for Jane's wedding. When all the children stood and sang at the service, many people were moved to tears. Following the wedding ceremony, Charles and Esther headed back to Eldoret to welcome more street children into their home and ever-growing family.

Six weeks later, on a Wednesday afternoon, Charles noticed a look of concern on Esther's face. "What is it?" he asked. "Is something wrong?"

Esther hesitated to speak. "It's, well . . . I hate to tell you this, but we have only enough food left for dinner tonight and breakfast tomorrow. After that there is nothing."

"Oh," Charles said. "And there's no money in our bank accounts to buy more."

"Now what?" Esther asked.

"We pray," Charles responded.

"Isn't it a bit late for that? Can we expect God to create food for hundreds of children out of thin air?"

Charles shrugged. "I don't know. He fed the Israelites in the wilderness, and Jesus fed the crowd with the loaves and fishes. All we can do is pray and trust Him."

Esther burst into tears. "It's so hard. What if it doesn't work? What if we've failed God and all these children?"

Charles closed his eyes and raised his hands. He was quiet for a long time, and then he prayed, "God, You have called us to this work. You said You are Father to the fatherless. We have enough food for two more meals. You know that. Please meet all our needs according to Your riches in glory. Amen."

That night as he lay in bed, Charles struggled with the future of the ministry he had been called to. The children—his children—many of whom he had rescued from starvation, might have to go without food in his home. Was this the beginning of the end? Charles slowly drifted off to sleep, praying that God would give him the strength to trust Him.

The next day Charles calmly went about his morning duties. He was counseling a boy in the backyard when several children rushed up to him.

"Daddy, Daddy, there's a big truck at the gate and a woman asking to talk to you," they said.

Charles was puzzled. He knew he had not ordered any new shipments. They didn't have the money to do so.

The children escorted him to the gate, where Esther was waiting for him. "I heard all the commotion," she said. "I wonder what's happening."

Charles saw a middle-aged woman standing beside a truck at the front gate. "Are you Mr. Mulli?" she asked with a smile.

"Yes, I am," Charles replied, "and this is my wife, Esther."

"How wonderful to meet you," the woman said. "I came as soon as I could. Last week I heard a woman at our church talk about you and all that you had given up for the street children. Then last night as I was going to sleep, I felt God telling me to hire a truck and load it with food for you. I hope you can use it."

Charles laughed with delight. "As a matter of fact, we can!" he replied.

"Come and see," the woman said, leading Charles and Esther to the back of the truck. It was loaded with sacks of maize, beans, rice, and many kinds of vegetables.

Charles shook the woman's hand. "Thank you from the bottom of our hearts. There is enough food here to last the children for at least three days. You have done an incredible thing for us."

The children unloaded the truck and carried the food to the storehouse. Before the woman left, she handed Charles an envelope. "This has been such an honor," she told him. "I mean, I got to meet the famous Mr. Mulli. It is so exciting."

After the woman drove off in the truck, Charles pulled out the envelope and looked inside. It was stuffed with money, enough to buy food for several more weeks!

Esther and Charles walked back inside hand in hand. "This is a miracle," Esther said quietly. "At the same time that we were praying last night, God was telling that woman to bring us food."

"Yes," Charles replied. "We must never forget that all things are possible with God if we believe."

It was a refrain Charles would come back to again and again as he faced more daunting challenges.

Chapter 11

Ups and Downs

Charles and Esther sat together in the doctor's office waiting for him to arrive. Charles had been to Eldoret Hospital more times than he could count accompanying sick children, but this time was different. This time Charles was here as the patient, to find out what was causing his tiredness and constant thirst. At first he just told himself he was working too hard. It was 1995, and in addition to driving to Ndalani once a week to supervise the boys and keeping the home at Eldoret functioning, Charles had enrolled in Bible college. He felt he needed more insight into how to help his adopted children in their own spiritual growth. Everyone told him not to work so hard and that it was no wonder he was tired all the time.

When the doctor walked into the office, Charles noticed his serious look as the two shook hands. The two men made small talk about the children before the doctor sat down at his desk and pulled a sheet of paper from the drawer. He glanced over it and then looked Charles in the eye. "You have diabetes," he announced. "Does either of your parents have diabetes?"

"No," Charles said, trying to take in the news.

"Your grandparents?"

"Not that I know of."

"Your children or siblings?"

"No, again," Charles said. "I can't think of a single person in my family who has diabetes. How did I get it?"

"Many times it happens when a person is overweight and unfit, but you're in great shape for a man of forty-six. Sometimes we don't know what triggers it."

The doctor talked on, but Charles found it hard to concentrate on what he was saying. The word *diabetes* kept pulsing in his mind. *I have diabetes? How can that be?* he asked himself. *I'm serving God, I have hundreds of children who are dependent on me, and I have diabetes?* He heard the doctor say, "If you don't look after yourself, we could end up having to amputate your feet or legs. Stress can also contribute to diabetes. You will have to slow down. If you follow all the directions I'm going to give you, take medication every day without fail, and get plenty of sleep, you will probably be able to live a somewhat normal life."

What did that mean? Probably? Somewhat normal? Charles's life was far from normal. He had many responsibilities to bear. Would he have to slow down or, worse, give those responsibilities up entirely?

Charles was still stunned at the diagnosis as he and Esther drove home. The couple sat in silence. They had nothing to talk about. Charles felt as though he had received a death sentence. He was slim and fit, and people often told him he had the energy of a twenty-year-old. But not anymore.

That night Charles stood beneath the stars in his backyard. "How could this happen to me?" he asked God. "I have so much to do—so much You've given me to do—and now I have an illness that's going to slow me down, maybe even stop me. The doctor talked about my legs being amputated. Is that in my future? How will I care for children if I have no legs?" On and on Charles prayed, focusing on all of the problems having diabetes would create for him. He stopped and waited. There were only questions, no answers, no clarity, no guarantee about how all this would end. *You have a choice right now,* he said to himself. *Either you can turn your back on God and refuse to believe that He loves you because He allowed you to get diabetes, or you can trust Him no matter how things look at the moment. Which will it be?*

A Bible verse, one Charles often quoted to the children when they were in trouble, came to mind: "Trust in the Lord with all your heart, and do not lean on your own understanding. In all your ways acknowledge Him, and He will make your paths straight."

"Yes, that's what I'll do, God," Charles said simply. "I will trust You. I have given You my body, my family, my wealth, everything that I have. I will not take it back now. I'm in Your hands."

For the first time that day Charles felt at peace. Yes, it was difficult to have a disease like diabetes, but he knew that God was still in control of his life.

Charles began taking medication to treat his diabetes and closely followed the doctor's instructions. As a result, the extreme tiredness he had been experiencing went away, though he still had to be sure he got enough sleep. He felt at full strength on December 31, 1995, when 220 second-grade through seventh-grade boys and girls from Eldoret relocated to Ndalani. Charles and Esther made the move with them, leaving behind a group of trusted workers to care for the children still at Eldoret.

In the eighteen months since the dedication service for the Ndalani property, the crew of seventeen boys and their teachers had worked hard clearing and preparing the land and erecting the first buildings. Charles was proud of their effort, especially since on many days the temperature had reached over 100 degrees Fahrenheit. The boys had never experienced such hot weather, since Eldoret had a mild climate. On some days, inside, under the corrugated tin roofs of the buildings the boys were erecting, the temperature soared even higher. But the boys and their supervisors stuck to the job, and now the other children had arrived to enjoy the fruit of their labor.

Life at the new home in Ndalani came with some hardships. There was no electricity on the property, and all the water had to be carried from the Thika

River. Nonetheless, the future looked bright for Mully Children's Family, or so Charles thought, but more challenges emerged.

Soon after the move to Ndalani, Charles was surprised to receive a summons to appear before the chief of the Kamba subtribe—the same man he had once asked to put his father to death for his misdeeds. Charles met with the chief in a tiny, dark room in the town center. The chief got straight to the point. "I am very disappointed in you, Charles Mulli," he said.

"How so?" Charles asked.

"You have brought criminals to our land, and not just any criminals, but criminals from other tribes. I have seen Maasai and Luo and Luhya boys and girls in town. We cannot have this. We know where they have come from, and we know what they are capable of. They are gang members and thieves and petty criminals. What were you thinking, bringing them here?"

"They have to go somewhere," Charles replied.

"Well, not here. You are a wealthy man, a man of honor in our community. When we heard you were returning to Ndalani, we expected you to bring your wealth with you—to help this community, not to add to our problems," the chief retorted.

"The children might have once been the things you say, but they are not like that anymore. They are changed," Charles said.

The chief scoffed. "You can't know that. None of us can know that. The people are very angry. They do not want other tribes on their land. They are going to run you off. I have called you to warn you. You should leave now."

"We're not going anywhere. The children need somewhere to live, and they will behave themselves," Charles said.

"Can you guarantee that?" the chief asked.

"Yes," Charles replied. "You can hold me person-ally responsible for any problems the children cause in town."

"Very well," the chief said. "I will tell the people and see what they say."

"Thank you. You will see. These children will be a blessing to us all."

"I'm not sure how that could possibly be," the chief said as he stood to leave.

As it turned out, the local people did make things difficult for the children but, thankfully, did not run them out of town.

In Eldoret the children had all attended the school Charles set up. Now, at Ndalani, Charles wanted to take the school to the next level. In Kenya, unless a school was registered by the government, enrolled students could not take the state examinations. The first of these national exams was held at the end of eighth grade, and if a student failed, he or she could not go to high school. Another examination was held at the end of high school, at which time a student had to make good grades in order to attend any college, university, or technical institute. Charles assumed it would be an easy matter to get his Ndalani school registered by the state so that the children about to enter eighth grade could take their exams at the end of the year. He soon found out otherwise.

The Machakos School District had 940 state-registered schools, all of which were attended by Kamba children. When Charles went to register his school, he was told by the school district officials that it was not possible. The officials told him that street children were impossible to educate and that if they registered his school and the children took the state exams, their results would bring down the average of the whole school district.

Charles knew that this was nonsense. His students were some of the smartest he had ever seen. They just needed a chance. He argued with the school district authorities, but they refused to budge from their position. "The Machakos School District allows for the education only of Kamba students," they said forthrightly.

The officials' unbending attitude shocked Charles. Surely street children had the right to be educated. Charles would not take no for an answer. A big part of the children's rehabilitation was the hope of a good education. Charles wrote to the minister of education in Nairobi asking for his school to be registered. He waited and prayed for a response. One week went by, then another, until only a week was left before the cutoff day when schools had to be registered by the state for the year. Charles waited anxiously. He was relieved when a letter arrived informing him that he could meet with the minister of education. But the meeting was scheduled for just three days before the registration cutoff date.

The entire Mully Children's Family prayed that things would work out. Charles was heartened by the fact that the minister of education was not from the Kamba tribe. Perhaps he would be able to look at the situation more objectively.

On the day of the interview, Charles drove to the minister of education's office in Nairobi. He was shown into the office, and Kalonzo Musyoka smiled at him as they shook hands. It was a good start. Charles smiled back. "What is the problem you are having?" the minister asked.

"I'm not able to register my school with the Machakos School District. I have nearly 240 children that I am educating there. They have already learned many things, and I want them to be able to go on with their studies. Some of them are very bright. Twenty-one students are in their final year of primary education and will soon be candidates for testing to get into high school."

The minister of education frowned. "Why won't they register your school?" he asked.

Charles hesitated. He didn't want to cause problems for the officials of the Machakos district, since that would make it harder to work with them in the future. "I'm not sure. You will have to ask them," he replied.

The minister picked up the telephone and asked his secretary to connect him to the education director at Machakos.

Although Charles could hear only one side of the conversation, it wasn't hard to tell that the minister of education was angry that the school district would not allow Charles's school to be registered. His voice rose to a yell as he reprimanded the school district officials for being so biased and ordered them to register the school for the coming year. It was all Charles could have hoped for. Now his students had to prove to the school district officials that they would not pull down the exam averages for the other schools.

With his school at Ndalani now running and registered with the state, Charles decided to move the remainder of the primary school–age children from Eldoret to Ndalani. This would leave seventy newborn to seven-year-old children, along with a number of workers, living at the property in Eldoret.

Charles also began strategizing about how to educate the students in his school past eighth grade. There was no high school to send them to in Ndalani. What they really needed was a high school to call their own. Of course, establishing a high school was a daunting undertaking. They would need professional teachers with degrees in many subjects, more buildings, equipment for the science labs, textbooks, and so much more. Still, as Charles prayed about the possibility, he became convinced that God would make a way for a Mully Children's Family (MCF) high school right on the grounds at Ndalani.

Charles called together two of his top primary school teachers, both of whom were qualified to teach at high school level, and asked them to start researching the idea. Soon three other teachers joined them. The plan they came up with was exactly in line with Charles's thinking. The boys would pitch in, using their carpentry, welding, and metalworking skills to help build the high school. One of the teachers taught technical drawing, and soon plans were drawn up for simple concrete-block buildings with plenty of ventilation to keep the students cool inside on the hot summer days. Following the plans, the boys began making windows, doors, and gates for the new buildings. Others calculated how much concrete, mortar, blocks, and stone would be needed, along with roofing material and wood. The only thing they lacked was the money to buy the necessary supplies.

Charles gathered the three hundred children now living at Ndalani, along with the thirty teachers who taught in the primary school. "I am here to tell you that God is going to provide us with a high school next year, in 1997," he said cheerfully. "Does anyone see a high school here?" He waved his arm at the vacant space to his left.

The children shook their heads.

"I can't hear you," Charles yelled, "so I'm going to ask you again. Does anyone see a high school here?"

"No!" the children yelled back.

"I don't either, not yet. But there will be one soon. God is going to give us our own high school. The biggest children have worked very hard to get to grade eight. Next they are going to go to our high school. God has already given you a mom and a dad, food, clothes, and a bed. Next he is going to provide a high school!"

The children cheered.

"Let's sing and thank God for what He is going to do for us," Charles said. They all sang several choruses, and then Charles dismissed them.

Within days, news that MCF was planning to establish a high school spread overseas. Donations began to arrive toward the project from people in various countries. With each new infusion of money, the high school project moved ahead little by little.

In January 1997, the results of the eighth graders' standardized national exams were ready. Charles and Jacob Otieno, Charles's right-hand man at Ndalani, stood staring at the sealed envelope. Had the street children pulled down the district average as everyone had feared they would? Charles took a deep breath and tore the envelope open. He felt goose bumps rising on his arms as he looked over the results and then handed the paper to Jacob.

Jacob read the results and stared at Charles. "God has done great things," he said, almost in a whisper. "This is incredible."

And it was. The Mully Children's Family school had ranked first out of the 940 schools in the Machakos School District, far outpacing any of the local schools.

"Can you believe it?" Jacob asked. "Our children are the best in the district, and they must be among the top in all of Kenya!"

Charles laughed. "They've worked hard. We've all worked hard. We gave them the opportunity, and they took it. I am so proud."

That evening the entire family at Ndalani gathered outside after dinner to learn the results and hear Charles congratulate the eighth graders, who had done so well. By now Charles had learned that their school had scored among the top one hundred schools in the country. They all danced in jubilation until the dust under their feet rose in a red cloud around them.

In the weeks that followed, many of the local people around Ndalani came to Charles to ask if their children could be enrolled in his school. How different this was from a little over a year ago when the locals had threatened to run him and the children out of town. Charles could not take all of their children. He was in the business of educating the neediest. However, he agreed to enroll sixty local children in the school who were orphans being taken care of by extended family. The school charged no fees, and the children went home each night. The situation gave Charles immense satisfaction. He knew how much it would have meant to him had he been offered free schooling and encouragement as a child.

By the start of the new school year in late January 1997, the high school was fully operating. As the year progressed, not only did the children in the elementary and high school continue to excel in their education, but they also worked hard in sports and music and gained recognition in those fields. Various MCF choirs competed in competitions, as did the karate teams. And MCF began winning trophies both in the local area and at divisional school competitions. MCF students also won the Yatta District science fair by developing a new type of animal feed made from soybeans that they had grown on the Ndalani property. They went on to compete in the national science fair finals. With each new accomplishment, the children celebrated by singing and dancing and giving thanks to God for their victories.

Chapter 12

"What You Have Done Is Quite Remarkable"

As 1997 progressed, Charles faced a daunting problem at Ndalani—clean water. All the water they used came from the Thika River that ran through the property. New children arriving often had difficulty adjusting to the water. Some would get sick from various waterborne bugs. But in October the water quality became a serious issue when two boys became ill and were diagnosed with typhoid. The river water was tested and found to be the culprit.

Charles did not know what do to. Over three hundred children were drinking contaminated water, and he wasn't sure how he could change that. The property had no electricity. Since there was no grid nearby to connect to, there was no way to power a water-purifying plant, even if they could afford it. The local elders told Charles that there was no underground water supply in the area. They knew this because over the years many people had tried to dig wells, which always turned out to be dry. Aware of this but desperate to do something about the situation, Charles hired a drilling rig and crew of drillers from Nairobi to come to the Ndalani property and see what they could do. The drillers sank two bores, each two hundred feet deep, but found nothing. The head driller shook his head and told Charles, "This area is as dry as a bone. You are wasting your money. There is no water down there."

At the same time, the condition of the two boys with typhoid became critical. Charles visited them in the hospital and prayed for their healing, but it was not to be. Both boys died. Charles was in the room when the second boy died. Seeing his adopted son lying lifeless on the hospital bed, he knew he could not rest until somehow the water problem was solved.

Charles began to pray constantly for God to intervene and provide a source of clean, fresh water on the property. "God, I know You didn't give me these children and lead us here for them to die from bad water. There must be a solution. I beg You, give us clean water."

For three days Charles devoted himself to praying for water. Then, at three o'clock on the fourth morning Charles awoke, his senses on high alert. He could feel goose bumps rising on the back of his neck. "Follow Me, and I will guide you to water," he heard a voice say. He wasn't sure whether it was just in his head or not, but the message was loud and clear. He woke Esther, grabbed a kerosene lamp, opened the door, and walked out into the moonless night. Esther followed, tying her robe as she went.

Charles walked straight ahead, then turned left and stopped. "Here is water," he said to Esther. "When we dig here, we will find water. God has just told me this. Let's give God thanks for providing for us." He took Esther's hand, and together they prayed and then returned to bed.

The next day Charles announced to the children that their water problems had been solved. There was water on their own property, less than a hundred yards from where they stood. The children cheered and danced. Their exuberance didn't last long, however. After the older boys had spent two days digging through the rock with pickaxes and shovels, they'd had enough. Some of the boys refused to dig anymore. "This is useless," they grumbled. "If a team of well drillers with big machines can't find water, how can we?"

On the third day, Charles's eleven-year-old son, Dickson, asked him to come to the hole. "We have reached the end," Dickson said as they both peered into the well. "We have hit the volcanic rock the well drillers told us about. You told us to dig. We have been digging for three days. There is no water. You say God told you to dig here. What do we do now?"

Charles could see the confusion in his son's eyes. He had only one answer. "We must keep digging. God told me this is where the water is," he said.

Slowly Dickson climbed down the scaffolding into the hole.

About an hour later, Charles heard yelling. *"Maji, maji* [water, water]! Dad, Mum, come quickly!"

Charles ran to the hole, surrounded by children who had heard the commotion and leapt up from their schoolwork. Instead of calling them back, the teachers ran with them. At the edge of the hole, Charles looked down. His two sons, Isaac and Dickson, were standing ankle deep in water, splashing it on each other and laughing. Charles hugged Esther and joined in the laughter. "God has answered our prayers!" he yelled above the excited voices.

The children gathered around and started chanting "maji, maji" as they clapped their hands and danced. Charles and Esther joined them. Now the family would have clean water. The well was soon prepared and capped and a water tower built. They named the hole Jacob's Well.

Soon afterward, an American visitor was so impressed with the work of Mully Children's Family that he offered to pay for electric lines to be run to the property and for the buildings to be wired for power. Now, in short order, the children had both clean water and electricity. These two additions allowed Charles to begin the next phase of his plan. Until now, the only gardening they had been able to do involved a two-and-a-half-acre plot where they grew corn. The plot was plowed by a team of oxen, and Charles knew it was time to modernize.

Charles and his seventeen-year-old son, Kaleli, walked the length and breadth of the Ndalani property and dreamed of what kind of agriculture could be possible. Charles decided on a large garden. The garden would allow him to employ and pay struggling local women to tend the crops. Such an enterprise would also provide food for Mully Children's Family, and if all worked out, there would be produce left over to sell.

At the start of the following year, Kaleli began attending Nairobi University, where he studied business and agriculture. Charles looked forward to learning about the latest agricultural techniques from his oldest son. Meanwhile, work on developing a larger garden began.

With the water problem solved, Charles was surprised when another strange sickness presented itself at Ndalani. Some children who became sick with seemingly simple illnesses, such as measles and the flu, failed to fully recover.

By now, various church groups from Canada and the United States were sending medical mission teams to help care for the children and the local residents. One of the doctors who had come to help suggested that the sickly children be tested for HIV/AIDS. Twelve MCF children tested positive for the disease. In response Charles set up a home for the twelve back at the property in Eldoret where they could receive special medical care.

Charles asked the doctors many questions about the disease and learned all he could about this new threat. What he learned scared him. He realized that millions of Kenyans were putting themselves at risk of getting HIV/AIDS, yet no one was talking about it. Charles made some charts and began visiting local schools, churches, and village gatherings to educate people about HIV/AIDS and explain how they could protect themselves from it. He then trained two social workers to carry on the work.

Amid the grim diagnosis of HIV/AIDS among some of the children, there were also things to celebrate. In 1999 the high school boys made it to the divisional soccer championship. Sixty boys, with five teachers accompanying them, were transported to the site of the championship on a large trailer pulled by one of the MCF tractors. Charles was there to wave them off and wish them all well.

Three days later, when he was visiting Eldoret, Charles was delighted to receive a telephone call informing him that the boys had won the championship, beating 123 other schools in doing so. It was a heartwarming moment for him. He could only imagine what the other schools thought of this motley crew of boys from many different tribes all working together to win. He hoped their success would spur other schools to also accept students from different tribes.

That was not what happened, however. Charles received a phone call from Jacob telling him that the boys had been ambushed on their way back to Ndalani. About two hundred boys from the two nearest schools had put rocks on the road to stop the tractor and trailer. When the MCF boys got down to remove them, they were attacked with knives and rocks. Charles could only imagine the scene. Not only were the MCF boys in top physical shape, but also they knew how to street fight, and they excelled in karate. "Even though they were outnumbered by more than three to one, our boys were unstoppable," Jacob reported. "By the time the police arrived, several of the attackers were badly hurt and the rest had run away. Not one of our boys was hurt."

Charles didn't know what to say. He was proud that the boys had won the soccer championship. He was proud that they had the skills to ward off their attackers, but he didn't like them using their karate moves to hurt anyone.

After the phone call, Charles got into his car for the six-hour drive back to Ndalani from Eldoret to talk with the boys. It was hard to know what to say to them, and he prayed for wisdom as he drove. He didn't want the fight to overshadow the boys' amazing sports accomplishment. They had a right to feel proud of that. When Charles reached Ndalani, the sixty boys who had been attacked gathered to hear what Daddy Mulli had to tell them.

"Did we do the right thing by fighting?" one of them asked. "I think I broke someone's thigh bone. Is that okay?"

Charles looked at each of the boys, who seemed genuinely conflicted.

"I am proud that you are not the kind of boys who go looking for a fight anymore," he told them. "Jesus has changed your hearts, and you love others. But yesterday you did fight. I understand that two hundred boys attacked you and threatened to kill you.

You had a right to fight back and save your lives. You know that we need to respond peacefully whenever we can. We need to forgive and to find a way to reconcile with those who want to fight us, but I understand that you did not have time to consider that. I am just glad that none of you were hurt."

Charles paused for a moment, marveling at the scene. Here was a group of boys who had been gang members and street kids, and they were struggling with the concept of fighting back to defend themselves. Once they would not have even questioned such action. What a long way they had all come as members of Mully Children's Family.

"Let me see your trophy!" Charles said with a broad smile. "And congratulations. You are the best soccer players in the district. Perhaps one day some of you will play for Kenya. I want to shake each of your hands for a job well done, and then I believe we have a party ready for you."

The boys cheered.

During 1999 MCF produced a bumper crop from their garden. With a steady supply of water and electricity to run irrigation pumps, more and more land was being used to produce food. That year they harvested tomatoes, kale, cabbages, and watermelons.

Charles was so proud of the quality of the produce they harvested that he took some of it to an official in Nairobi to ask if it would be possible to export some of what they grew to Europe. That was where the big money in growing produce lay. The official was so impressed with what they had grown that he came to Ndalani to see the operation for himself.

"You know," the official told Charles during his visit, "the biggest profits are in growing and exporting French beans. So far only large corporations are doing it because the rules are so tough, but if there is any way that you could pass the new European Union regulations for growing and transporting produce, you could make a lot of money to help support these kids."

Charles ordered a copy of the European Union regulations and began to read them. Growing French beans and exporting them to Europe was a daunting task. There were rules for everything—from planting, fertilizing, and watering to picking, packing, and shipping. Charles and the farming team met together to work their way through all the regulations.

French beans turned out to be a challenging crop to grow. Eventually MCF mastered the art of doing so and felt that they had properly implemented all the necessary regulations. Charles decided it was time for an inspection by EurepGAP, a global partnership to promote safe and sustainable agriculture. A group of EurepGAP auditors from the Netherlands arrived at Ndalani to spend a day going over the entire process of how the French beans were grown. When they had finished their inspection, they met with Charles. The head auditor handed him a wad of papers.

"You got some things right, but not much," the auditor said matter-of-factly. "Your overall score was 10 percent." Charles was too shocked to think of anything to say. "Here is the list of violations. Your biggest downfall is poor record keeping, but there are many other violations as well. You are using pest control chemicals that are not approved by Eurep-GAP, and your irrigation system is not up to our standards. You could try correcting these problems, but it's unlikely any operation your size would ever meet our standards. It takes a European-based corporation to truly understand what we're after."

"Thank you," Charles mumbled as he took the report. "I want to learn how to do better."

That night at the dinner table, Charles announced the bad news to Esther and some of his biological children. "It is not a good result," he told them. "I do not recall ever getting 10 percent in anything I've tried to do. It would be easy to give up. But we teach the children to not give up, to learn from their mistakes, and to keep going. That's what we're going to do. We will apply dedication and perseverance to this task until we master it. There's a lot at stake here. When we get the certification, we will be able to get top money for our beans. Then we can hire more women who need jobs and help support the children as well. Now is not the time to give up."

This was easier said than done. Charles and the MCF team had to locate the right pest control chemicals, educate the workers on how to clip their fingernails and tie up their hair, completely redo the pipes and joints of the irrigation system, and make vast improvements to their record-keeping system.

One month later Charles asked the EurepGAP auditors to come back for another inspection. Once again the inspectors spent the entire day with clipboards and pens, writing, measuring, and questioning. At the end of the day, the head auditor came to Charles. "Many smaller farms like yours apply for export status. It is a very difficult thing to get. You know how strict our policies are."

Charles looked at him, trying to gauge what he meant. He could not read the man's face.

"Here are the results once again," the auditor said, handing Charles another wad of paperwork. "I'm very impressed and happy to tell you that you have a score of 98 percent this time. You will be allowed to export your beans to Europe." Then he shook his head. "What you have done is quite remarkable. We would like to invite other farmers to see what you have implemented here. They could learn a lot from you."

Charles felt a giant smile spread across his face. "Yes, yes, of course. We would be happy to host anyone who wants to learn. Thank you!"

That night, the whole Mully Children's Family celebrated. They had persevered and overcome together.

As the year went on, the family had more to celebrate. Charles was honored with the Robert Pierce Award from World Vision International for outstanding work in humanitarian and Christian service to the poor. In deciding who would receive the award, the organization looked at the difficulty of the situation being addressed, the quality of the program, and the number of people being helped. By then there were nearly five hundred children in Mully Children's Family at Ndalani and Eldoret, and Charles still sought more desperate children who needed help.

Chapter 13

Sinking into Violence

It was 2001. When the telephone rang, Charles answered it.

"Hello," came a voice at the other end. "You might not remember me. My name is Duma, and I visited your family at Ndalani last year for the agricultural field day."

"Yes, of course I remember you. How are you?" Charles responded.

"Very well, thank you. I was impressed with what I saw on the visit—we all were. I happen to have two hundred acres of land in the Yatta district, seven and a half miles directly southwest of your property at Ndalani. It's on the main road and about six miles from the national park. I want to sell half of it. Would you be interested in buying it? I'm going to retain half the property, but I am getting ready to sell the other half."

"Yes, we are interested, but we don't have the money at present. Can you call me again in two weeks, and we can discuss this further?"

"I can do that," Duma agreed.

When Charles hung up the phone, he prayed. "Father, You know our needs. You know I have been wanting to establish a separate place for those street girls who are pregnant or already have small children of their own. This property sounds ideal. Please show me what to do."

That night he discussed the idea with Esther. Her eyes shone as she talked about the possibilities. "Just think of it, Charles. It is close to Ndalani but not too close. Many of the street girls will be tempted to go back to their old lives, so it's good that it's out in the country." The two of them talked long into the night, dreaming of programs to help the girls become good mothers, learn trades such as hairdressing, carpentry, accounting, and dressmaking, and learn how to take advantage of microfinancing opportunities.

Within a week Charles received an email from a man in Canada who wished to remain anonymous. The man wanted to donate money to MCF, an amount large enough to cover 40 percent of the cost of the Yatta property. Charles emailed the man back to ask if the money could be used toward helping establish a facility for street girls and their babies. The answer he received was yes. Charles let out a whoop of joy. He was confident he was on the right track—God's track—in wanting to buy the Yatta property. He called the owner back and told him he could make a down payment on the land. The deal was soon done, and work began on the property immediately.

Charles wanted the new home for the street girls built as soon as possible. Workers and finance flowed into the project. Church groups from all over the world sent money to help pay off the debt on the land and provide building materials for classrooms, dormitories, and a dining room. Every time Charles worked at the property to help set up the site, he prayed for the girls who would soon be moving there from Ndalani.

A year later, in 2002, Charles was granted the Angel of Hope Award from World Vision, in part for his work with the street girls at Yatta.

The following year, Duma, the previous owner of the Yatta property, visited Charles to see what he was doing with the land. He was so impressed with the way the MCF social workers and teachers were working with the pregnant street girls and those with small children that he gave the hundred acres of land he had been keeping for himself to Charles. This could not have come at a better time. Charles had big plans for the Yatta site, and now with two hundred acres he could do even more.

By now French bean production at Ndalani was in full swing, with an average of eighteen hundred pounds harvested each day. Most of the beans were exported to France. In 2003 an Australian businessman named Teagan Jones toured the Ndalani property. Over lunch he turned to Charles and asked him what his next step would be.

"A greenhouse," Charles replied. "A big greenhouse covering two and three-quarter acres in which we can grow crops all year. French beans mature here in six weeks. With a greenhouse we could get eight crops a year and keep the women we employ working year-round. It would also help us to be self-sustaining, and that's something we want very much."

"All right, Charles, I'll do it. You shall have your greenhouse," Teagan said.

Charles wasn't sure what to say.

Teagan smiled and went on. "Put the details on paper and send them to me, and I'll see to it you get the biggest greenhouse you've ever seen. You can grow all the French beans or anything else you want to grow in it."

"That's a lot of money," Charles said.

Teagan laughed. "You have a lot of kids to take care of. I think you could use a little help, don't you?"

Charles laughed too. "Thank you," he said. "This means a lot to our family."

By the end of the year, another businessman, this time from Canada, offered to pay for greenhouses at Yatta. Again, Charles looked at this as an opportunity to provide jobs for more local women and earn extra income from the produce for his ever-growing Mully Children's Family. And this time the greenhouses would cover twenty-five acres of land. The water that ran off the greenhouses when it rained would be captured and used for domestic duties and irrigation. As part of the installation of the new greenhouses, five dams were constructed to hold the projected 5.5 million gallons of runoff rainwater.

Soon the work on the new greenhouses at Yatta was complete, and lush rows of French beans and other vegetables filled them and the greenhouse at Ndalani. When the rainwater runoff had filled the reservoirs behind the dams at Yatta, a fish-farming operation was also begun, raising catfish and tilapia.

It seemed to Charles that with God's help everything he put his hands to seemed to flourish. By 2004, when MCF held its fifteen-year anniversary, 440 children and young adults were living at Ndalani, 90 babies and younger children at Eldoret, and 50 teen mothers and their babies at Yatta. MCF also ran a home and hospice for children who were sick with HIV/AIDS and other serious illnesses.

Over a span of fifteen years, the lives of more than sixteen hundred children had been dramatically changed. In fact, the MCF school was still rated number one in the district. And from the school's first graduating class, a number of the children had received university scholarships to train as doctors, lawyers, and diplomats.

One of the accomplishments Charles was proudest of was the way all his children got along. He constantly reminded them that they were brothers and sisters regardless of what tribe or region of Kenya they came from. But one day this family spirit was to be tested to the breaking point.

"Dad, you must come and look at this," Isaac called from the open cafeteria outside Charles and Esther's room.

Soon Charles, Esther, Grace, Mueni, and Isaac were all staring at the television. "Kenya appears to be sinking into a violent state where no one is safe," a commentator said as scenes of bloody violence flashed across the screen. The images were almost too much for Charles to believe. It was January 1, 2008, a day when the country should have been celebrating the New Year along with the rest of the world. It was also four days after the most contentious election in Kenya's history, and the country had erupted into tribal violence.

Since Kenya had gained its independence from Great Britain in 1963, long-standing problems had existed between the Kalenjin and the Kikuyu tribes. After independence, when white settlers left their fertile farmland in the White Highlands of central Kenya and the Rift Valley, the Kikuyu tribe, who had won the majority of the seats in Kenya's new parliament, redistributed most of this land to members of their tribe. The problem was that before Europeans came and settled this land, it had belonged to the Kalenjin and the Maasai people. Now, following the 2007 election, political commentators were accusing President Mwai Kibaki of rigging the elections so that his party, the Party for National Unity, or PNU, would stay in power. President Kibaki and his cabinet were mostly Kikuyus. Members of the opposition party, the Orange Democratic Party, cried foul. When their cries were not listened to and President Kibaki was declared president once more, they began to riot on the streets of Nairobi. The unrest quickly spread north into the Rift Valley.

Charles and his family watched footage on television of Kikuyu homes in the Rift Valley with the words "Leave Your Place Today or You Will Be Killed" painted on the outside walls. Mobs of teenage Kalenjin boys had taken the law into their own hands and appeared ready to slaughter thousands of Kikuyu people in the Rift Valley.

Then came the most chilling news of all. A TV reporter announced that over fifty unarmed Kikuyu women and children, some as young as a month old, had been burned to death while taking refuge in a church in Kiambaa. Charles and Esther looked at each other. Kiambaa was a suburb of Eldoret, less than ten miles from the MCF home there.

"Thank God none of our children are there," Esther said with tears in her eyes. "God was good to warn us."

"Yes," Charles agreed.

Two weeks before the election, Charles had visited Eldoret and had become aware of the mounting political tension enveloping the place. As he prayed about what to do, he felt he should temporarily move the children and staff from there to Ndalani, in case things got out of hand. Now he was glad he had done so. He had suspected there could be unrest over the election results, but what was unfolding in the country was unimaginable.

The television coverage of the unrest and violence continued. There were reports of police shooting people in the streets and mobs boarding buses to check IDs. Anyone who did not belong to the mob's tribe was hauled off the bus and killed by machete.

Charles could not watch any more news reports. "Let's take a break," he said. "I'm going for a walk. We need to pray for guidance."

Charles walked beside the Thika River. He had many choices to consider regarding how to respond to the situation. They could try to flee with the children at Ndalani and Yatta. The Tanzanian border was 120 miles away, but where would the food come from to feed so many children if they left? After all, they cared for over twelve hundred children now. And what about the three hundred staff?

As Charles prayed, the fear that had engulfed him watching the news reports evaporated. It was replaced by a sense of peace, a sense that everything would be all right. He knew that God would protect the children at Ndalani and Yatta and that he needed to go to Eldoret to see what MCF could do to help the families being affected by the violence there.

An hour later Charles was back at the house when he received news that the farmhouse and all the storage buildings of MCF in Eldoret had been burned. He called all the children and workers together and told them what was happening in Kenya.

"We are being torn apart by tribal violence. You know you are all from different tribes. Some of your best friends are children from tribes that are fighting each other at this moment. But we here at Mully Children's Family belong to a much bigger tribe— the tribe of Christians. That is what holds us together. We do not fight. We love and serve each other. We are family. You are my children, and I love you all. God wants us to love each other and to love our neighbors as ourselves."

Very early the following morning, Charles prayed with his family and then set out for the airport. It was too dangerous to drive all the way to Eldoret because of the many roadblocks that had been set up. And with no official government in place, chaos reigned in the country.

When Charles arrived at the airport, the place was busy. People stood in small groups or walked silently, terror etched on their faces. Charles knew that many of them were making potentially life-or-death decisions. Should they head into the worst areas of violence to be with their families or stay where they were and hope their loved ones got out?

Charles made his way to the Fly 540 airline counter and asked for a ticket to Eldoret.

"There's one left on the nine o'clock flight," the agent said. "Do you want it?"

"Please," Charles replied, pulling out his wallet.

Charles boarded the twin-prop, eighteen-seat aircraft for the fifty-minute flight. No one spoke much, and all eyes were on the ground below them as they flew. As the plane passed over the town of Burnt Forest, Charles saw houses ablaze and people running to and fro. In the distance, plumes of smoke rose over Eldoret.

After the airplane landed in Eldoret, Charles grabbed his bag and headed to where a line of taxis would normally be waiting. Today there were just a few. The drivers were all Kalenjin—tall and lean.

Charles walked over to a taxi and opened the door. "Can you take me to the Agricultural Society of Kenya Show Grounds where the IDP camp is being set up—the camp for internally displaced people?" he asked.

The driver nodded. Charles climbed into the backseat. The taxi eased away from the curb and out onto Kitale-Cherangani Road. As the taxi moved along, Charles saw broken windows, smoldering buildings, and corpses on the side of the road. The scene was beyond anything he could have imagined. Roadblocks were manned by men with spears and machetes.

The driver coasted to a stop at the first roadblock. Several armed Kalenjin men stood in the roadway. The driver wiped his brow with a handkerchief and took shallow breaths. *He's very nervous*, Charles thought. *I should be the nervous one. He's Kalenjin too, and the tribes are not killing their own people.*

The driver tried to roll down the window, but he turned the handle the wrong way, applying more and more pressure until the end of the winder snapped off. Then he turned what remained of the winder the other way.

"ID," one of the men in the road said, waving his bloody machete at them.

The driver shook like a leaf as he reached into his pocket. Charles took a deep breath and prayed, "God, don't let them see me. Let me pass straight through here." His last name Mulli would give him away as a member of the Kamba tribe as soon as he showed them his driver's license.

The man with the machete took the driver's ID

and walked over and showed it to another man, who read it and nodded.

"Okay," he told the driver. "You can go through. Welcome."

No one had said a word to Charles.

As they drove on, Charles said to the driver, "You seemed very nervous back there. Was there some kind of problem?"

The driver let out a bitter laugh. "I'm Kikuyu. I have a false ID. If they knew who I was, I'd be dead."

Charles was shocked. The man looked Kalenjin. "You are taking quite a risk," he said.

"We all are," the driver replied. "Death is everywhere."

The taxi arrived at the Agricultural Society of Kenya Show Grounds, where Charles had been many times before to see various displays and demonstrations. Today, however, he barely recognized the place. The grounds were filled with white canvas tents.

Charles paid the driver, got out of the taxi, and began walking up and down the rows of tents. Children sat in the mud crying for food. Mothers stood around them with blank faces. Some of them still had blood on their clothes. Some people sobbed, but most were eerily silent.

Charles met with the Red Cross manager in charge of the camp to request permission for MCF to assist the children now living there.

"Why do you want to be registered as an assistance provider? What can you do for the people here?" the manager, who sounded American, asked.

Charles took a deep breath. He knew that what he was about to say would sound crazy. "I want to provide food for the children, and teachers so the children can resume their education. And we will bring school supplies for them and provide counseling for them and their families. They really need that."

The man stared at Charles. "Yes, they do. They need all of those things, and it is wonderful of you to offer, but in truth, do you think you can provide all of that? There are over thirty-five hundred children in the camp."

"It is a lot," Charles agreed, "but I believe it is the right thing to do."

"It may be the right thing, but can you do it?" the Red Cross official pressed. "Let's say you want to feed all of the children. It is very difficult to obtain food at the moment. You are not a magician. Where will you get it from?"

"I don't know yet," Charles said, "but we have trusted the Lord before, and He always provides."

"Okay," the manager said, sounding less than convinced. "Let me get this straight. Are you coming to ask us to give you food so that your organization can distribute it here, or are you saying you will provide the food yourself?"

"God will provide the food," Charles said. "He's done it for us before. Then we will use it to help the children here. Please give me the opportunity, and you will see. I will provide cooked food for all of the children in the IDP camp."

"So you're not asking us for money or food?"

"No, absolutely not," Charles replied.

The Red Cross manager walked a short distance away and talked in quiet tones with several other workers. Then he returned to Charles. "Okay, I will give MCF a permit to work in the camp, but I have to say, if you manage to feed and provide schooling for all of these children, it will be a miracle."

Charles reached out to shake the manager's hand. "I agree," he said. "My God is in the business of miracles."

At six that evening Charles headed to the airport for the trip back to Ndalani. He had been in Eldoret for only nine hours, but it felt to him like a lot longer. He had seen enough gruesome scenes and suffering to last a lifetime.

At Yatta the following morning, Charles called together the members of his biological family who were there. They were all subdued, waiting to hear what he had to say. He told them briefly about what he had seen and then said, "I have made a decision, one that will affect all of us as a family. I obtained a permit for MCF to work in the internally displaced persons camp, and we're going to go back to Eldoret and do whatever we can to help the children there and their families. Are you with me?"

One by one they nodded, first Isaac, then Ndondo, Mueni, and Grace. What a difference twenty years had made. Charles thought back to when he first decided to take in street children and how his own children had resisted so much. Now they were ready to risk their lives to help him.

"The children in the camp need all the same kinds of help that we offer to the children here. They have been through great trauma. Many of them have seen family members killed. They have experienced much violence and hatred. At the camp, you, Isaac, will get a computer system up and running and keep it that way. Ndondo, you'll work with me maintaining communication with friends and churches around the world and with the workers and children back here at Yatta and at Ndalani. Grace and Mueni, you two will be in charge of finances and procuring food, fuel, water containers, and educational supplies. Does that sound okay to all of you?" Charles asked.

One by one the Mulli children again nodded in agreement.

The Mulli family spent the next two days preparing a sixty-five-member team of people to go to Eldoret. The team received training in dealing with people in trauma and fasted and prayed for the task that lay ahead of them. A week after Charles's return to Ndalani, the team was ready to depart for Eldoret. Food and supplies were loaded onto the bus, along with the team, which included Charles and Esther. Charles had arranged for heavily armed Kenyan police officers to ride inside the bus with them all the way to Eldoret. Once the officers were aboard, the bus set off on the journey. As they traveled, Charles quietly prayed that God would take care of them all and keep them safe and that He would provide the supplies they would need to minister effectively at the camp. After a day of traveling, they arrived safely at their destination, despite a number of roadblocks and the roving tribal gangs they saw along the way.

Chapter 14

Changing the Land

The sixty-five team members crammed into the MCF compound in Eldoret that had once been the Mullis' home. The smell of smoke hung in the air throughout the city. That evening Charles held a special prayer meeting for the work that the group was about to undertake. Afterward he urged everyone to get a good night's sleep. They would be getting up early the following morning to head to the internally displaced persons camp.

The next morning, Mueni and Ndondo told Charles that they had seen a group of men attempting to scale the compound wall. But before the men could slip over the wall, someone on the street had fired a shot. There was shouting, and then the men scattered. Charles wasn't surprised. Eldoret was a very dangerous place to be at the present time.

After breakfast the team loaded huge cooking pots, firewood, and food supplies into the back of pickup trucks and drove to the Agricultural Society of Kenya Show Grounds, where the IDP camp was located. Although Charles had been there only a week before, the sight of thousands of hopeless people still shocked him. When the team arrived at the camp, they all set to work.

Charles divided the team in half. One group unloaded the large iron pots and food supplies and set up a kitchen, while the other group set up large tents to be used as classrooms. As the two teams worked, Charles and Esther quietly walked up and down the rows of tents, praying for the people inside them. They stopped at one tent that housed a mother and daughter. Charles stepped into the entrance.

"May we come in?" Charles asked. "My name is Charles Mulli, and this is my wife, Esther. We are here to see if we can help you in any way."

The woman nodded. The girl stared at the ground.

"Thank you," Charles said as he sat down on one of two stools inside. Esther sat on the other. "We would like to hear how it is that you came to be here," he said gently, giving the woman his full attention.

The woman opened her mouth to speak but instead started sobbing. Her daughter, whom Charles guessed to be about twelve years old, joined her. It was gut-wrenching as Charles and Esther waited while the two cried. When the woman had regained her composure, she said, "My name is Chinira. I am a Christian. My family are Christians. We were all huddled in the church at Kiambaa when the attack happened. They threw petrol on us and then the fire erupted. My husband escaped through a window, and I watched the mob kill him. Then my son suffered the same fate. My daughter and I escaped somehow."

At this the daughter let out a loud wail.

"It's okay, it's okay," Chinira said, hugging her daughter tightly. Then she turned to Charles and Esther. "My husband has been killed, my son is gone. I am not going to ask God why, but if there is anything you can do to stop my daughter's suffering, I beg you to do it."

The four of them, their eyes wet with tears, sat silently in the tent. After a while Charles broke the silence. "May I pray for you?" he asked.

Chinira nodded. Charles began, "Father, You know these precious children of Yours. I pray that You will come into this tent and comfort these suffering people. Let them feel Your love and hope."

When he opened his eyes, the girl began to speak. "I am Dalila, and I was in the church when it started to burn. I had my baby brother with me." Dalila's voice barely rose above a whisper as she told how when the flames came, she almost managed to get her brother to safety only to have him disappear at the last moment in the confusion of the desperate crowd. "I let him go," she sobbed, "and he is gone."

Charles let out a deep breath. "I am so sorry to hear that this happened to you," he said. Then he and Esther talked with Dalila about the certainty that her little brother was in heaven now, beyond all harm.

Then they challenged Chinira and Dalila to forgive those people who had done such evil against them.

"You will not be free or start to heal properly until you forgive," Esther said gently.

Charles knew how hard it is to forgive when someone has hurt you so badly, but Dalila was able to pray. She told God that she forgave those who had attacked the church and harmed them so deeply. Charles then invited Dalila to come to the MCF area, where she could get a meal every day and continue with her schooling. For the first time, Charles saw the girl smile.

As Charles and Esther stepped out of the tent, they braced themselves. There was so much suffering in this one tent, this one family. And there were so many other tents in the camp, each one, no doubt, occupied by people with equally heartbreaking stories. "Jesus," Charles prayed aloud, "guide our actions and make us a source of healing for these hurting, broken people."

Charles and Esther visited several other tents, listening to stories and praying with people. When they returned to the MCF area, they found hundreds of children who had already heard about them and were lined up waiting for food.

As time went by at the camp, each day the sixty-five-member team from MCF provided meals for 7,500 children and schooling for 3,500, along with trauma counseling and organized sports activities. Charles was particularly concerned for the orphans and those who were expecting babies.

More than a month after the post-election violence

had erupted in Kenya, former United Nations secretary general Kofi Annan came to the country to begin negotiations to end the tragedy. At the end of February 2008, he succeeded in getting the two opposing political parties to sign an accord that established a coalition government in Kenya. The violence subsided, but not before 1,500 or more people were killed and up to 600,000 were displaced. The members of the MCF team continued working at the IDP camp until December 17, 2008. During that time, they fed and taught the children living at the camp and worked closely with the Red Cross.

At the end of their time at the camp, Charles and Esther welcomed into their family 250 camp children with nowhere to go, stretching the number of children they cared for to over 600. Among those relocated to Mully Children's Family was Dalila. Her mother had asked Charles and Esther to take her, since she was not able to provide food or housing for her. Charles was overjoyed that they were able to give a fresh start to Dalila and the rest of the displaced children left behind.

During 2009, another tragedy befell Kenya— drought. Across much of the country the usual rains did not come. Crops began to dry up and wither, and livestock began to die from lack of water. The Eastern Province of Kenya, where the Yatta and Ndalani properties were located, was one of the areas hardest hit by the drought. The area around the two facilities had always been semiarid, but water from the Thika River and Jacob's Well at Ndalani and rainwater runoff at Yatta had always sustained those living there. This allowed the fields and greenhouses to be irrigated so that MCF could produce bountiful crops, even when the rains were late or less than expected.

In 2009, however, things were different. No rain at all fell, and before long the normally fast-flowing Thika River, one of the larger rivers in the country, completely dried up. It felt odd to Charles to be standing in the bottom of the river on dry sand and rocks. At any other time, he would have been completely underwater. No one in the district could ever remember the river drying up like this. To make matters worse, as the drought continued, Jacob's Well also dried up. Now Charles was forced to send a tanker truck to Nairobi each day, a four-hour round-trip, to fetch water.

With no water from the Thika River to irrigate, the crops began to dry up and fail. The normally green fields turned a dirty shade of brown. The situation became desperate. Charles called all the children and staff at Ndalani and Yatta together so that they could all pray for rain. For hours on end, they knelt and prayed, but still the drought continued unabated.

Charles had to bring in not only water from Nairobi but also food to feed the ever-growing Mully Children's Family. But buying food in the middle of a drought was expensive.

In the area around Ndalani and Yatta, approximately forty thousand people lived on farms and in small villages. Charles soon learned that hunger was rampant among them. Most families ate only once a day and sometimes skipped a day's meals to conserve what few food supplies they had on hand. As a result of their hunger, many children began missing school. Charles knew he had to respond to this need. He decided to provide one hot meal a day for the neighboring children throughout the area. Each day, on average, one thousand children made their way to MCF for a meal, some of them walking six or more miles to get there. Sometimes a child would be accompanied by a hungry parent or guardian. Charles fed them all, and as the people sat and ate, he moved among them, talking to them and telling them about God's love.

Charles spent many hours in prayer, praying not only for rain across the country but also for the money to pay for the desperately needed food and water. As news of the drought and famine in Kenya spread around the world, people began donating money to MCF to help sustain them through the challenging time.

Although MCF fed the children from the surrounding area one hot meal a day, Charles knew that he also needed to help their parents and other family members. He organized a day when MCF would donate food supplies to families in the surrounding community. To Charles's amazement, ten thousand people showed up to receive maize, beans, and flour. It took some quick planning on the part of the MCF staff to get everyone organized and in line. First, those who came were given a hot meal, and then the food supplies were distributed to them. It took four hours to distribute all the food to the crowd. To keep order, Charles had to continually reassure those at the end of the line that there was enough food and water for everyone.

During 2009, in the midst of the drought, Charles received two honors. He was awarded an honorary doctorate degree in humanities by the United Graduate College and Seminary in the United States. With the conferring of this degree, he became Dr. Charles Mulli. He was also given the Head of State's Commendation for his service to his fellow citizens through MCF. This award was bestowed on him by Mwai Kibaki, the president of Kenya. While Charles appreciated both honors, receiving awards was not the reason he did what he did. He did it because he believed that God had told him to do so, and there was a lot more to do.

From the beginning, Charles had looked for ways to make Mully Children's Family self-sustaining. At the house in Eldoret, they had begun growing vegetables in the yard. Not only did this help feed the children, but the children also learned new skills as they tended the garden. Now at both Ndalani and Yatta, large-scale farming and market gardening operations were going. Both properties had vast greenhouses in which produce could be grown year-round. This helped to feed the children and generated income for MCF through the export of French beans to Europe. And the fish farm at Yatta was still flourishing.

Charles wanted to do more. Yet the drought demonstrated just how dependent they were on the climate, especially located in a semiarid area as they were. Charles realized that the land hadn't always been that way. Once the area around Ndalani and Yatta had been much greener and the climate milder. However, over the decades, as a result of human activity, most of the trees in the area had been cut down. This had led to two things: soil erosion when it rained and an increase in the temperature as the area turned semiarid. Charles decided that if the actions of people could so drastically change the climate of the local environment over the years, determined human activity could change it back. He decided to turn his attention to creating a microclimate around Ndalani and Yatta that would provide a cooler environment and create more rain. This would make the land more productive, not only for Mully Children's Family, but also for all those living in the local area. To create this microclimate Charles turned to trees.

Trees had been planted on the two properties from the beginning, mostly for beautification purposes and to act as windbreaks for the crops in the fields. But as the drought began to abate and water returned to the river and well, an intensive tree-planting operation got under way on the two properties. The operation initially involved two particular drought-resistant, fast-growing trees, grevillea and senna. Large swaths of land were set aside on both the Yatta and Ndalani properties. The children and others who came to help and learn about conservation and taking care of the land set to work. They didn't plant just a few trees. In all, they planted nearly four million trees on the two properties. And as Charles envisaged, a microclimate began to develop and change the area. Clouds formed above the glades of trees, and it rained regularly. The trees also brought down the temperature, making the area around Yatta and Ndalani cooler. The once arid, brown land turned lush and green.

Charles was so encouraged by the success of the tree-planting operation that he partnered with Norwegian Church Aid to replicate the microclimate change in other parts of Kenya. A tree nursery was established at Yatta to produce a million saplings a year to be freely given away for planting in other regions of the country. In 2010 Charles was awarded a certificate from the United Nations Environment Programme, recognizing his efforts at making a tangible difference in the environment of Kenya.

This new focus on environmental conservation and tree planting led to the establishment of a charcoal production facility at Yatta. Over the years, most trees in Kenya had been cut down to be used as firewood. But with the new focus on tree planting to produce milder microclimates, not just around Yatta and Ndalani, but also throughout Kenya, Charles reasoned that he needed to produce an efficient fuel people could use for cooking without having to cut down trees. That fuel was charcoal. Not only was charcoal a more efficient fuel, but also it didn't produce the same amount of carbon dioxide as wood when burned, thus helping to cut back on greenhouse gas emissions into the atmosphere. Charcoal was already being used in most of Kenya's large cities. However, those living in the countryside did not use it. Instead they resorted to cutting down trees. Charles hoped to change their habits.

In 2011 Charles received his second honorary doctorate, this time in social work from the Kabarak University in Kenya. Daniel arap Moi, the chancellor of the university and a past president of Kenya, personally conferred the degree on Charles.

Spurred on by local and international interest in conservation, Charles developed an ecovillage at Yatta, complete with solar, wind, and biomass energy sources. MCF started the annual Renewable Energy Awareness Day to showcase what they were doing and how it was impacting the surrounding community for good. They also offered help and advice to those interested in starting their own environmental improvements.

Of course, Charles was delighted that the children in Mully Children's Family were grasping the importance of taking care of and nurturing their environment. He was also delighted with their other achievements. The MCF karate team became the karate champions for Kenya and went on to scoop the East and Central African trophies. The MCF children continued to graduate from high school with high marks. The MCF high school consistently ranked in the top ten high schools in the country, and around one hundred students a year went on to the next level of education at vocational colleges, technical institutes, and universities.

In 2014 Charles turned sixty-five years of age, and Mully Children's Family celebrated the twenty-fifth anniversary of its founding. But Charles showed no signs of slowing down. That year he received a Transform Kenya Award in the education category. The aim of the Transform Kenya Awards was to recognize and celebrate those people who, through innovative approaches, were doing remarkable things to improve the lives of Kenyans. As he accepted the award, Charles reminded himself that he still had a lot more to do. He had more innovative approaches to institute, not only for the members of Mully Children's Family, but also for Kenya and Africa.

Chapter 15

"Always Continue Doing Good"

Toward the end of 2014, Charles's father, ninety-one-year-old Daudi Mulli, became ill with cancer. He was hospitalized in the intensive care unit in Nairobi in February 2015. By then MCF had established a permanent office in the capital city. Charles chose to work from there so that he could visit his father several times a day.

On March 4, 2015, Daudi asked Charles to bring all of his brothers and his mother to the hospital. As they gathered around his bed, Daudi, whose cancer had spread to his lungs, making it difficult for him to breathe, rallied himself and half sat up.

"I will be leaving soon," Daudi said. "I am passing the baton to Charles. I want you all to listen to him. He will take you to a higher level. You must live

179

in peace together and act as a family. Then God will bless you and your children and grandchildren."

As Charles stood by his father's bedside, he marveled at how much he had grown to love and admire the man. In the years since his father had become a Christian, God had transformed him from a stubborn and cruel man into a loving father. Daudi had learned how to interact with others and truly care about them. Many people told Charles how loving and kind his father was. Daudi had been elected an elder in and a chairman of his village church and spent many hours each week encouraging young people in their faith.

Two days later, Charles visited his father during his lunch hour. As usual he stood quietly beside the hospital bed. After a few minutes his father woke up and said, "Ah, you are here."

"Yes," Charles replied.

"There are people pushing me to go on a long journey, but I do not want to go until I have told you to always continue doing good things for the people. Continue to help the children. Continue to lead. Do not give up. Help the poor."

After a pause, Charles asked, "Is there anything you want me to tell the people?"

"No, nothing else. This life is a journey, and now I must complete mine," his father said.

Tears welled up in Charles's eyes and spilled down his cheeks as he kissed his father goodbye. At five o'clock that evening, Charles received a phone call from the doctor saying that his father was not doing well. He hurried to the hospital, but Daudi had died by the time he got there.

As Charles drove back to his office, his mind flashed back to when he was a child and afraid of his father coming home drunk every night, afraid that his mother would die after a beating. He remembered his family repeatedly abandoning him and refusing to help him when he was a small boy with no support in the world. He recalled how he had struggled to feed and educate himself. Most of all, he thought of the time he had called his father before the subtribal council and had watched as Daudi was lashed by the young men. Another five minutes and his father would have been dead. But something had made Charles intervene and plead for his father's life. Charles also recalled how, after the visit to the witch doctor, Daudi had slowly come to realize that he was serving the wrong spirits, that the Spirit of God was far more powerful than the spirits of his ancestors. After this, Charles had seen his father and mother blossom into a kind, compassionate, and godly couple. His parents had spent many hours together praying for the work of MCF.

Daudi's funeral was an event like no other. In accordance with Kamba tradition, it was held in his house, though the people soon spilled out onto the street. Over three thousand dignitaries, church elders, farmers, and children stood side by side in the hot sun. Charles spoke about how our lives can be likened to a marathon. Some people, like his father, might not start off strong, might falter and lose their way, but can still finish strong.

"It doesn't matter," Charles said, "that you have never done well. What matters is that you finish strong and that you keep moving forward in faith. In life, success is measured not by the humbleness of your start but by the greatness of your finish. My father finished his race as a great man. I do not feel like my father has really died. He has gone on before me to meet Jesus, and one day I will follow him."

After the funeral service, Daudi was buried on his plot of land. The family then went back to the MCF property at Ndalani to eat dinner together. It felt good for Charles to be with his biological children. They were all grown up now, and every one of them had a degree except Isaac, who had an IT diploma. Half of them were married, and between them they had given Charles and Esther ten grandchildren— seven granddaughters and three grandsons.

Over dinner the Mulli family talked about the past and how the older children remembered when Daudi had become a Christian and then a wonderful grandfather. They talked about the present—the three thousand children now in their care and the ten thousand they had cared for who were now grown up and had "left home."

Mully Children's Family now had seven operating locations in Kenya. The original location in the Mullis' old home in Eldoret still operated, with a focus on rescuing orphaned and vulnerable children in the Rift Valley and the western provinces of the country. Most of the children rescued through the work in Eldoret were relocated to the Ndalani or Yatta facility to live. These two locations functioned as the main centers of operation for MCF.

Close by was another facility, located at Kangundo, which ran as a drop-in day center providing free primary education, food, clothing, medical care, and spiritual counseling to orphaned children in the area who lived with grandparents or other family members. In Vipingo, a rural slum located near the coast, just north of Mombasa, MCF had a facility that worked with needy boys and girls, many of whom had been abused. This location dispensed free meals and an ongoing education program. Many of the girls currently being rehabilitated at Yatta were from this area. A location in the Kipsongo slum in Kitale was situated north of Eldoret near the Ugandan border. This facility provided free meals and primary education to needy children in the slum.

MCF's newest base of operation in Kenya was currently being established in the far north at Lodwar in Turkana County, near Kenya's border with Ethiopia and South Sudan. This area of the country was arid and prone to droughts and famines. It was also one of the most underdeveloped areas in Kenya. Poverty and illiteracy were rampant, as was a lack of basic services such as hospitals and schools. Charles was excited about this new location. He looked forward to MCF providing free food and education, along with clothing and clean drinking water, to the needy and vulnerable children of the area.

Mully Children's Family had also opened a branch in Dar es Salaam, the largest city in neighboring Tanzania. As the Mulli family talked about the future, Charles contemplated his next dream—creating a

Christian university at Yatta to serve the MCF students and the poor of Kenya. His plan was that the
courses taught would be focused on training young
people to become leaders in Kenya and other areas
of Africa. The school would offer courses in agriculture, the environment, conservation, renewable
energy, education, social development, and entrepre-
neurship. Thirty percent of the positions in the new
school would be reserved for very poor students who
would have no other hope of attending university.

Late that night after the funeral service and dinner, when everyone else had gone to bed, Charles
and Esther went outside. They sat quietly for a long
time looking up at the spectacular night sky. Charles
broke the silence. "It has been quite a journey, these
past twenty-five years, hasn't it, Esther?"

Esther smiled and turned to him. "It has, but God
has led us."

"Yes," Charles agreed, "and it's not over yet. The
university is our next big challenge. Are you with me
in it?"

"Yes," Esther replied.

Charles laughed. "You know the biggest hurdle
of all is getting other people to understand the vision
God has given me. Some people, even Christians in
our organization, are negative about it. They say we
can't hope to get three thousand students attending the university. But I believe God will bring them
around, and then we'll go on as a team, together."

"I believe too," Esther said, reaching for his hand.

Charles smiled at her. "We must keep praying
until it comes about, Esther. Prayer is the work. All the

rest is results. The last thing Daudi told me before he died was 'Always continue doing good things for the people.' With God's help, I'll never stop doing that."

If you would like more information about the ongoing work of Mully Children's Family, please visit the following websites:

- For information about Mully Children's Family Kenya: *MullyChildrensFamily.org*
- For information about Mully Children's Family support activities in the USA: *mcfus.org*
- For information about Mully Children's Family support activities in Canada: *mcfcanada.org*

You may also want to watch the recently released documentary *Mully*, directed by Scott Haze, to learn more about Charles and his family.

Bibliography ────────────────────────────

Boge, Paul H. *Father to the Fatherless: The Charles Mulli Story*. Castle Quay Books, 2007.

────. *Hope for the Hopeless: The Charles Mulli Mission*. Castle Quay Books, 2012.

Material for this book was also derived from extensive interviews between the authors and Charles Mulli in Siesta Key, Florida, and Atlanta, Georgia.

Janet and Geoff Benge are a husband and wife writing team with more than thirty years of writing experience. Janet is a former elementary school teacher. Geoff holds a degree in history. Originally from New Zealand, the Benges spent ten years serving with Youth With A Mission. They have two daughters, Laura and Shannon, and an adopted son, Lito. They make their home in the Orlando, Florida, area.

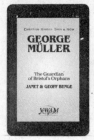
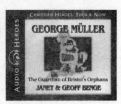

Also from Janet and Geoff Benge...

More adventure-filled biographies for ages 10 to 100!

Heroes of History

Christian Heroes: Then & Now

Available in paperback, e-book, and audiobook formats.
Unit Study Curriculum Guides are available for many biographies.
www.HeroesThenAndNow.com